MW01614729

Journey in the Fields of Forever

John Harricharan

Other books by
John Harricharan

When You Can Walk on Water, Take the Boat
Morning Has Been All Night Coming
Remembering and Other Poems
The Power Pause
Under the Tamarind Tree
Intuition – Your Guidance System
You Can "Live Long and Prosper"

And Others

MORNING HAS BEEN ALL NIGHT COMING

PRINTING HISTORY

New World Publishing edition published
Berkley edition 1991 (six printings)
Editor Pensamento (Portuguese) edition 1993
HarperCollins (UK), Aquarian edition 1994
Luciernaga (Spain) edition 1995, 1996, 1997,
1998, 1999
Amrita (Italy) edition 1997, 1999
Amrita (France) edition 1997, 1999
Turkey, Romania and Other Countries
Being printed and reprinted in many other
countries as recently as 2014

First edition copyright © 1994 by John
Harricharan
This edition © 2014

ISBN: 978-0-943477-37-4

A John Harricharan Book®™
John Harricharan books are published by the
New World Publishing Company, a division of JHH
& Associates, Inc.

Dedicated to

Malika Elizabeth and Jonathan Nian,
who exhibit, to a great degree, the innocence of
children and the wisdom of the ancients.

Special Thanks

My gratitude to Anita Bergen for the many hours she spent assisting me in bringing this manuscript into a readable form.

Special appreciation to my brother, David Harricharan, whose support and encouragement were constantly felt. Had he not been my brother, I would have wanted him for a friend.

With great humility, my eternal gratitude to Robert "Butch" James who made it possible for this book to be published. Every once in a long, long while the world is blessed by the presence of a soul such as Butch. I am doubly blessed to be able to call him my friend.

And thanks to Sri Vishwanath, Pandeyji, Yanni Maniates and other dear friends for also joining me in the "Journey in the Fields of Forever."

Table of Contents

Foreword

Perhaps, in the never-ending search for meaning, not only does meaning seem to elude us, but we find ourselves faced with the eternal questions of life. Why do roadblocks always appear at the most inopportune moment? Where is help when we are down in the arena and boots are on our necks? Why am I here and where am I going? Will I ever again see my loved ones who have died? And so it goes ... on and on. Although no one could satisfactorily answer such questions, there is something deep within each one of us that whispers hope and says that no matter how dark the way and how deep the snow, the paths of glory lead ever onward and all roads finally lead home.

This book is the story of a journey in living. The characters reveal to us a sense of joy and yet, at the same time, we feel their pain. This book is about you and me, about our constant, endless quest for that which seems unreachable. Some of us have already met in previous books such as *When You Can Walk on Water, Take the Boat* and *Morning Has Been*

All Night Coming. Others of us will meet here for the first time and continue together on a fascinating voyage which leads through the fields of forever.

As the world spins on with dizzying speed into the future, we find ourselves caught up in the uncertainties of our times. But such uncertainties are not new. They have always been with us since the days our ancestors roamed the wild, prehistoric plains and they will always be with us in the future. What we must do is reinterpret the way we look at the world. Perhaps, then, we may find that life is biased on the side of good, that difficulties have a way of passing, that change is a constant and that we are all children of an infinitely, wise and benevolent God.

With new meaning and understanding, we will find the world to be a much friendlier place, our home away from home. Then will we be able to stand calm when the lightning strikes, to be patient in the midst of the storm and to be centered in the midst of chaos. All roads lead home. May you enjoy the adventures in the Fields of Forever.

John Harricharan

Chapter One

The Return of Gideon

Somewhere between New York and London at 39,000 feet above the earth, my heart was at peace while my exhausted body and mind took the opportunity to rest. I had just successfully completed a one-week, business trip, which had taken me from one coast of North America to the other, then over the Pacific to down under in Australia. Mission accomplished in a few days, it was back to the United States and then over the Atlantic to London.

Now I was returning home, filled with anticipation at soon being able to see my children again, of the thought of relaxing on the porch, of watching the birds and squirrels in the backyard and myriad other less demanding, winding-down activities. It will be good to be home again. Sooner or later, we all return home.

The chorus of turbine engines exerted a hypnotic hum as we hurtled across space. Unlike most other recent flights, this one was a pleasure to be on board. It was relatively uncrowded. Less than fifty passengers occupied the belly of this big bird, which is usually accustomed to hosting more than six times that number.

It crossed my mind that airlines generally are not pleased with flights that are so empty. Yet, that was precisely what I wanted — empty seats to my left, empty seats in front of me and still more empty seats behind me. No crowds, no fuss, no bother, no one kicking the seatback, no incessantly chatty traveling seat-mates, just a quiet, peaceful flight back home. I adjusted the seat, leaned back a little farther and settled myself into a more comfortable position.

Somewhat, as if in a dream, my mind began to wander the hallways of time that took me through the hopes and dreams of yesteryear. I have always loved flying, though not as a pilot but as a passenger. And not in little insect-like planes but in giant birds of the sky like 747's and 767's. Personally speaking, awaiting departure at an airport was akin to a mystical experience. Planes, for me, meant travel and travel led to faraway places. Since my earliest childhood, my fascination with faraway places had never ceased and, perhaps, never will.

I recalled my first flight as a teenager leaving one country for another to continue my education. The excitement of foreign adventures was mixed with the sadness of leaving my family. As the plane took off and the northern coast of South America dropped below the horizon, I remember brushing a small tear off my cheek, yet smiling at the glorious possibilities of exploring a new, fascinating and sometimes frightening world. It would be years before I would see my family again.

I don't sleep much on airplanes and I read very little when up in the air. High above the clouds enveloped in this meditative environment, I much prefer to reflect on the nature of reality, to philosophize and luxuriate alone in my thoughts. Today was no different as I reflected on the past week. Indeed it was a grueling one. My body's bio-clock was indecisively choosing among time zones across three continents, but my mind, at ease on an uncrowded flight, was drifting among the clouds of yesterday and tomorrow.

Yawning, I glanced through the window again. If you leave London in the late afternoon flying westward toward New York, you would experience a prolonged twilight period. It's as if you were racing after the sun, never quite catching up as it drops into its nest in the west, leaving you to sleep or gaze hypnotically in its spell.

Another yawn as I glanced again at the clouds. There weren't many of them, but they appeared to come to life changing shapes and evolving into new, intriguing forms, ever so slowly, ever so peacefully as we sailed overhead. Here was one that resembled a giraffe, long neck, spots and all stood out against the pale blue sky. And over there, another cloud took the shape of an acacia tree, complimenting the giraffe on the African landscape. Lower and somewhat farther to my right was one shaped like a car — a Volkswagen beetle no less.

Clouds hold a special attraction for me, especially when I'm flying above and can enjoy them from this unique perspective. They seem so angelic, so pure, so easily shaped into sculptures of the imagination wherein one can read all sorts of strange tales. I watched the Volkswagen beetle cloud as it began shifting its form into wispy little alphabet letters. At first, vapory patches seemed to break away and almost disappear before my eyes.

This strange cloud seemed to have a will of its own, changing shape again. How amusing! It may have been the angle or a trick of the light. Parts seemed to be forming the letters... G...D...N. Then they vanished, changing forms like some animated caricatures in the process.

It is fascinating how the analytical computer of the mind connects random thoughts and pictures to other thoughts and experiences of the past. The letters GDN following the Volkswagen cloud brought to mind a half-forgotten incident of long ago where I had seen the name GIDEON on the license plate of a Volkswagen.

Mind accessed memory banks and connected the dots as I recalled the adventures a mysterious friend of mine named Gideon shared. His friend Marla was no less mystical than he was and under their tutoring and guidance, I had learned much about the higher perspectives of the confusing experience we call life. So strange and mysterious were their appearance and behavior that at times, I didn't even believe that they really existed! Yet, I have with me, to this day, the books* in which our earlier adventures were chronicled.

As we moved through time into evening and through space toward the east coast of North America, I recalled how I first met them and what remarkable personalities they were. Through the tough times of the past, from the loss of all my material possessions through the death of my wife, Mardai, and from a condition of utter despair to a situation full of promise, Gideon and Marla would appear in an almost magical fashion to administer a sorely needed dose of hope and spiritual vision, then, just as magically, disappear. They were truly angelic beings come to earth.

It had been a number of years since I last saw them. We were sitting on the back porch discussing a letter they'd brought me from a friend. Since then, no word, no communication, no sign from either one of them. It was almost as if eternity itself opened up and swallowed them forever. With these thoughts in mind, I pressed the button for a flight attendant. I had the greatest urge for a steaming cup of coffee.

When You Can Walk on Water, Take the Boat and *Morning Has Been All Night Coming*

It couldn't have been more than a few seconds before a flight attendant came up the aisle from behind carrying a cup of hot coffee on a tray. As I started to inquire if he knew how to read minds, he stated in a vaguely familiar voice, "Your coffee, sir. Just as you like it. And to set the record straight, I haven't been swallowed by eternity, I just live there." I looked up with a start to see who this was, only to behold my long lost friend, Gideon. I nearly knocked the coffee off the tray, then just sat there, jaws wide open, staring in disbelief at the broadly grinning face of Gideon.

He offered me my drink and said, "I didn't mean to startle you," and continued matter-of-factly with, "You didn't think we were through with you, did you?"

After the initial shock of seeing him, the first words to leave my mouth were, "Gideon! Is this you? I mean ... I was just thinking about you and Marla. What are you doing here? How did you...?"

Before I could finish the sentence he put his hand on my shoulder and said, "It's been a long time. Do you mind if I sit and we'll catch up on what's been going on?"

"Please, please sit. Tell me, where have you been and what have you been doing?" I inquired as he slid into the seat next to mine.

"Well, did you miss me?" he teased as casually as you please.

"Of course I missed you," I replied. "You and Marla just disappeared one day, and the way I figured it you must have died, because I never heard from either one of you again. It's been years, Gideon. You *do* have this habit of disappearing for years and re-appearing in a most unexpected manner."

"I certainly didn't die, as you can clearly see. I've just been away doing other things. But it's time to visit with you again, to finish the work we started ages ago. Tell me, John, what have you been doing since our last meeting?"

I was a thousand questions as I stared at him. He did not seem to have aged at all. He still sported the well-trimmed beard and his sparkling eyes spoke of untold mysteries. This time he was dressed in a flight attendant's uniform with two medals pinned over his breast pocket. "I was thinking about you just moments before you appeared. What are you doing working as a flight attendant?" I asked, deliberately ignoring his question.

"It was the best way to meet you again. At least we'd be able to chat for a while, exchange thoughts and bring you up to date on what's going on. Why do you think the flight is so uncrowded? We requested a special plane for you. Do you think this was all by accident? A mere coincidence? No accidents in the universe, John. Just choices, lots of them and each choice produces a result which creates further choices. Frustrating, isn't it?"

"Who requested a special plane?" I asked.

"Oh, Marla and I, of course. Who did you think?"

"Where's Marla? Is she on this flight too?"

"No, not on this flight, but temporarily in the airline business. You'll see her soon enough. Do you have many more questions?"

"Yes! I do. I always have lots of questions. And you haven't answered most of them yet, Gideon." Again I wondered whether I had fallen asleep and was dreaming all this when Gideon lowered his voice and spoke in a more serious tone.

"Most of your questions will be answered in time," he said. "Right now, I'm just supposed to tell you that Marla and I will be working with you again.

Glorious adventures ahead, John! Now tell me about the children. How are they doing?"

I always had the impression that he knew most things, but here he was asking me about the children. Didn't he know? Perhaps, he was just trying to start a conversation. "The children are fine," I replied, "Jonathan will be in college soon and Malika is going on to graduate school. Their mother would have been proud of them, Gideon. We talk about her often, you know."

"She *is* proud of them and in many ways assists you in helping them to learn and grow. Do you think that you accomplished such an enormous task without any help?"

"I didn't mean it that way, Gideon. But their mother died years ago and we have struggled and sacrificed to survive and get to this point. The struggle hasn't been easy. It certainly hasn't been a picnic, but overall, we're doing OK. Don't you know all these things, anyway? You always seem to know everything."

"I did get some reports and I did stop by from time to time just to peek in, so to say. Well, I'll be in much closer contact now. I'll be seeing you soon to continue our work." Gideon stood up, smiled at me and continued speaking as he turned to leave. "Marla will meet you when your flight lands. I have to go now."

Before I could respond he was gone. Just as in the past, he simply walked down the aisle turned and disappeared. Overcome by a yawning fit, I turned and stretched. Not very convincingly, I told myself I must have fallen asleep; I probably dreamed this whole scene about meeting Gideon again. But in front of me on the foldout tray were the two empty coffee cups Gideon and I had used. No, it wasn't a dream. He really had returned.

Chapter Two

A Near-Life Experience

I glanced at my watch, noticing we had less than an hour or so before touch down. Dinner had just been served, but I had no desire for airline food. Not far from the airport is a café-style restaurant where I frequently stop when I travel. I thought I'd stop there on my way home and grab a bite. Seeing Gideon again after all these years had rekindled in me a great curiosity about life.

Much had changed since the first time I met him. While on a business trip, his car had broken down in our office parking lot. Since then, our friendship evolved into a student-teacher relationship. The ideas he'd shared continually served to remind me of the unlimited beings we are, if we could only believe.

Since those early days, the population at large had developed a much broader awareness of things unseen. Simultaneously, technology had advanced at such a rapid pace that even in the most remote corners of the world, one could watch the Olympic Games or witness a courtroom trial as it occurred.

Countless books about the human spirit were written, causing many bookstores to expand their section devoted to spirituality. The media rediscovered the existence of angels and thus, angels were reborn on the human plane. In some of the most credible media, past lives and future lives were explored until one could meet an army of past-life Caesars, Cleopatras and kings and queens in any programming time slot.

It appeared that a blend of spirit and commerce enriched the bank accounts of many astute entrepreneurs who were quick to grasp the concept that the "poor in spirit" would pay royally to really "see God." Authors, mystics, gurus and group leaders proliferated and brought ideas of a New World employing their newfound methods. Some spoke of a specific number of steps that were necessary for enlightenment. Others pointed out insights that were discovered in faraway lands under mysterious circumstances. And still others, in quiet, humble voices, whispered the cry of the ancient Hebrews, "Hear ye, O Israel, the Lord God is ONE!"

New Age prophets and their religious teachers spoke of various convergences and impending disasters around the turn of the century, of fire and earthquakes, famines and floods. And then there were those charismatics, wiser in the ways of the world of commerce than their more esoteric cousins, who preached the gospel of "the laws and the profits" and all their brethren were amazed at how well they prospered.

And so it was as the jet neared the coast of North America, I reflected on the ways and means of humankind. Throughout the years, Gideon's guidance had given me a workable perspective of life and living. Instead of spending too much time on "Near-Death Experiences," he had preferred to instruct me on the joys of "Near- Life Experiences" as it related to our present journey here on Earth.

The prospect of learning from Gideon once more brought a feeling of great excitement and anticipation. I certainly could use some help and advice in numerous areas of my life. "The times, they are a'changin'" has been true since time immemorial. The only permanent aspect of the universe is change and our ability to be successful and happy is directly proportional to our ability to adapt to and work within change.

The voice on the cabin speakers at that moment brought me back to reality. "We will be arriving in a short while. In preparation for landing, please bring your seat backs to the upright position and return all trays to their locked position. Make sure your seatbelts remain fastened. It has been our pleasure serving you and if your future plans call for air travel, please consider flying with us again."

I complied with the request and then turned around, glancing up and down the aisles, hoping to catch another glimpse of Gideon. He was nowhere to be seen, which did not surprise me since appearing and disappearing seemed to be old habits of his. I gathered my personal belongings, packed them away in my flight bag and prepared for arrival.

The touch down was as smooth as silk. If you were not aware that it was happening, you might not have even noticed. That's how it goes sometimes, just like in real life, one minute up in the air, the other down on the landing strip without so much as a bump to let you know you've arrived.

A few minutes later as we pulled up to the gate I turned, half hoping to see Gideon again. But he wasn't there. Deplaning and passing through Immigration and Customs are relatively simple matters, especially if you don't have too much luggage. I only had one suitcase and a carry-on, so I hurried to the carousel to claim the suitcase.

On some flights and at certain airports, reclaiming your luggage can take almost as long as the flight itself. Unfortunately, this seemed to be one such occasion. Most of my fellow passengers had already recovered their belongings and left, while I was one of the last ones remaining. Patience is a virtue I've been pursuing all my life. While I'm considerably better at it now than in my youth, it still requires tremendous determination and effort on my part. Finally, after about twenty minutes of grumbling under my breath, I marched toward the luggage counter to inquire.

Focusing on the frustration of the moment, I hadn't glanced around as I pondered how much better I could run airlines, specifically, baggage claim departments. A voice from behind a huge support column startled me. "John! John!" it exclaimed, "are you looking for your luggage?"

I snapped around to see who had called my name. Not thirty feet away, next to my suitcase, stood one of the most beautiful baggage handlers I had ever seen. From under the official "Red Cap" her long, golden hair fell in streams of sunshine over her shoulders. A glowing smile decorated her face and her blue-green eyes were dancing mischief as, haltingly, I approached.

"For goodness sakes, John!" her voiced fairly rang with delight, "you really don't recognize me!" and she threw her arms around my shoulders as she gave me the most delightful hug I'd received in a long time. And then I knew. How could I not have recognized her sooner?

"Marla!" I fairly shouted, "it's you! I didn't notice you at all. You're so... so beautiful. I didn't expect..."

"What?" she interrupted, "do you have anything against a long-time friend meeting you at the airport? Gideon told you I'd be here, didn't he? Sorry I hijacked your suitcase for a while. Couldn't resist the prank. You always look so amusing and childlike when you're puzzled."

"Like an amusing child, eh? Just how I want to appear. And yes, now that I think of it, Gideon did mention that I'd be seeing you again soon, but I didn't think it would be this soon and here. What's this? You two working part-time for the airlines now?"

"No" she replied, "we're still with the old company—G & M Enterprises. But let's not stand here, let's go have something to eat. I'm sure you know a place that serves that greasy stuff you like."

Knowing her, I didn't even bother asking how she knew what I had intended. During the years I've known her and Gideon, they always seemed to have this uncanny ability to guess with great accuracy, what I wanted to do. I followed her through Customs as she pulled my wheeled suitcase. I offered to carry my own luggage but she laughed and said, "I'm the baggage handler today. Relax, you've had a long flight."

"I need to flag a cab," I said as we walked up to the curb.

"Not to worry, John. I'll see that you get home after dinner. Here's our limo now."

The driver got out, took my suitcase and hand luggage and placed them securely in the trunk while Marla and I slid into the back seat. A short while later, we were deposited at my favorite little café and settled ourselves in for dinner. I was looking forward to talking with her again.

After placing our orders, I leaned back in my chair and looked straight at Marla. "You haven't aged a day since I last saw you years ago," I said. "As a matter of fact, you look even younger."

"A matter of perspective, John," she replied. "You're as old as the hills or as young as a newborn day. It all depends on you and how you perceive your world. You don't see things as *they* are, you see them as *you* are."

"Then if I'm seeing you as I am, I must be in pretty good condition myself," I said with a grinning wink.

"Much better than you want to give yourself credit for," she replied.

"Thank you," I laughed.

The waiter brought our meals and as we dined I asked, "Tell me, Marla, what are you and Gideon doing here? Why are you here again? Oh, I'm happy that you're back, but I'm also very curious. Is this another lesson-learning period? You know how I hate lessons and exams."

"The final lesson, John," she said in a more serious tone. "A lesson that's a bit different from the ones you learned years ago. Now let's just enjoy dinner—savor the present moment. Too much focus on near-death experiences; let's enjoy a 'near-life' experience."

I sat across the table, relishing my dinner while, at the same time, silently watching the light play soft fireworks in Marla's hair. The conversation drifted from remembrances of times past to possibilities of the future without touching too deeply on the reasons for our meeting again. Perhaps, not everything has a reason. Perhaps, some things just are.

There we sat, two friends who were worlds apart and yet, so close. One who seemed to transcend the normal worries of time and space and the other who spent most of his waking hours making a living instead of making a life.

As the last of our dinner plates were cleared, Marla beamed that radiant, sunshine smile again. "You must be anxious to get home, to see the children and rest after such a grueling week," she said.

"Yes, I miss them very much. And I do need some rest. Around the world in a week or so could be rough."

Over my objections, she paid the tab and we walked hand in hand to the waiting limo. "James will drive you home," she said. "Sorry I can't come with you this time, but maybe soon. Give the kids a big hug for me. And here's a special one for you."

She moved closer and placed a gentle kiss on my right cheek. There in the moonlight with the cool breeze blowing through our hair, I said good-bye to Marla. I knew I'd be seeing both her and Gideon again, soon.

It wasn't too long before the limo pulled into my driveway and I was home. Yes, all paths lead back home. The sailor returns from the sea and, as the poet said, the hunter home from the hills.

Chapter Three

A Quiet Afternoon

My first few days back home were spent going through mail, returning phone calls and playing catch-up with what was happening while I was away. Marla and Gideon were a pleasant memory and I somewhat relegated them to the background of my mind, especially since I knew they would be visiting occasionally.

The children and I spent quite some time together chatting about what was going on in their young lives. Jonathan kept me busy with questions and arguments about the world and how it worked. Always the happy-go-lucky one, he was a delight to watch as he involved himself with the "affairs of state" as he saw them. Spontaneity and kindness were his watchwords. Had I submitted a computer request for the ideal son, I couldn't have received a better one.

Malika never ceased to amaze me with her wisdom and concern for others. Generally the more serious one, she made sure that everything was always in order and that all tasks were accomplished on time. Had I prepared specifications for the ideal daughter, I couldn't have done better.

And I? I attempted to play "Solomon," the referee in residence, as I presided over who was right and who wrong in their seemingly endless squabbles. Most time, playing the part of diplomat, I negotiated compromises to keep the peace. Now as I regard it from the perspective of today, I wonder how I ever survived. Yet, I think I learned more from this pair than from all others combined.

It has always been a source of amazement and consternation for me to watch them grow. I remember so well the years when I'd bring home two identical toys of different colors, one red and one blue. Of course, they would both want the blue or both ask for the red. They fought for the same seat in the car and for the same things when different ones were available. But television shows? That's where the differences began. They both wanted to watch different programs at the same time on the same TV. For some strange reason, to them, my TV set, my stereo, my VCR always seemed infinitely more enjoyable than their own.

Their mother would have really been proud of them. Especially since her death, the bond forged by the three of us was extremely strong. We delighted in simple pleasures, like a family barbecue on the back porch or just gathering around the kitchen table commenting on the latest news. Sometimes when I look at them, I realize that our children come to stay with us for only a very short while. Obvious as it may seem, everyday they are with us is one less day we have them. Eventually they must go their own way, blaze their own trails, make their own mistakes and reap their own consequences, even as we ourselves did.

This particular evening, I was quietly sitting at the kitchen table, reading a new book a friend had sent me and sipping away on a mug of coffee when the phone rang. I picked it up, only to hear the voice of Gideon saying, "Hi John! Just wanted to see if Marla and I could visit with you? We're in the area and could get to your home in about fifteen minutes."

"Sure, Gideon. That would be great. The kids are out for a while, so I don't have any 'daddy' things to do right now. By the way, I saw Marla the other day. Hate to say it, but she looks a lot better than you do... ."

"I know, I know," he interrupted with feigned sadness. "She said you didn't look bad yourself, either. We'll be over in a few minutes."

Gideon's visits, especially when Marla was with him, were always unpredictable. You would never know where the conversation would lead nor what would happen next. The coffee had not even finished brewing when they arrived. There was a knock at the door separating the kitchen from the porch and I peered through the glass at the smiling faces of Gideon and Marla.

Ushering them inside, I greeted them warmly and seated them at the kitchen table while I poured a round of coffee.

"Well," I asked, "what are you doing in this neck of the woods? I know you just didn't happen to be passing by? You must have something specific in mind—that's why you're here."

"He seems to know us only too well, Marla," Gideon said with a wink. "But then again, John, we don't always need a reason to see you. Friends, no matter where they are, love to get together just for the fun and enjoyment of each other's company. You're a dear friend of ours and we love your company."

"If you love my company so much, how come I haven't seen either of you in years, except for last week, of course?" There was a noticeable edge of sarcasm in my voice.

Marla responded, "It's like this, John. Both Gideon and I were temporarily called away on another assignment. There were others who remained to assist you when needed, but we had to leave for a while. We did keep up on the reports about you and learned that you'd managed to come through some very difficult times. However, we knew you'd always come through any difficulty."

"I always assumed you knew about my situation. And of course, the moment I finished struggling with one problem, there were bigger and more difficult ones to deal with." I looked from one to the other waiting for a reply.

"That's how life is, John," Marla said. "You finish one grade and then you pass on to another. You learn to count from one to a hundred, then from a hundred to any number. Then they teach you the multiplication tables followed by simple but basic principles of mathematics. Later come algebra, geometry, calculus and others. You could quit school if you wanted to, but you'd still have to go into something else. Anyway, why are we spending this gorgeous afternoon discussing such things? Tell him what we had in mind, Gideon."

Gideon took another sip of coffee, leaned back in his chair and looked at me through half-closed eyes. "It's been such a long time since we've done any fun things together. Marla and I have checked with others in the company and they've all agreed that we should take you along on one of our travels. Even the Chief thought it'd be a good idea."

"A trip? Super! I'd really love that!" I said, bubbling with anticipation. Those who worked for him always referred to the President and Chairman of the Board of G & M Enterprises, the company Gideon and Marla worked for, as "Chief". We had met a number of times in the past and I would love to visit with this amazing personality again.

"But tell me more, please," I continued. "How is the Chief? Where will we go? When can we start? Will I be able to have a meeting with him? You know, like the ones I had years ago? Come, come, tell me!"

Both Marla and Gideon burst out laughing. "One thing at a time, John," he said. "We'll get to all your questions, but one at a time. First, the Chief sends his regards. Most times, he sends them directly to you, but he said something to the effect that often you mistake them for junk mail or are too busy to notice. And sure, we'll go on a trip or two."

"That sounds great! It's been quite a while since I've been on a vacation. I'm anxious to get started. Tell me more! Will the children come too?"

"Not now for the children," said Marla, "they have other things to do. And in their own way, they are familiar with some of what we'll be doing. Remember that we're all connected by bonds that span eternity itself, so your children, we, and others of us are related in wonderful ways. Many of us know the same things and help the others to remember."

"I remember the trips we took long ago. The learning experiences, the adventures. I can't wait!"

"Our idea is to help you find," said Gideon, "the great secret of life. There is only one secret of life. And it's really not even a secret, since it's been around for a long time. We'll tell you where to find it and, perhaps, how to use it. It's simpler than you think."

"That's one of the main reasons we're back with you," said Marla. "There are other reasons, of course, but this is by far the most important. By the time we're finished with these adventures, there'll be no need for us to work with you in this way and you'll go on to finish the task you had set for yourself. You'll sing your song, you'll accomplish your mission, you'll fulfill your destiny, so to say."

"*One* secret you say? Only one? Aren't you aware that as we approach the end of the millennium, there are those who talk about ten methods, fifteen steps, various insights or 'Eleven Secrets of the Universe'? Even Moses had ten laws." I looked really smug as I said that.

"Yes, yes, I know that," replied Gideon, "but let's not get too involved in details at this time. Eventually you'll understand what we mean."

"Gideon," I said, looking him straight in the eye, "I wasn't going to bring this up at all, but I have this overwhelming urge to ask. I also know that I've asked this before, but I've got to ask again. It's been a number of years since Mardai died. Naturally, the children and I still miss her very much. Sometimes we feel her presence close to us. Does either of you know where she is and what she's doing? There are times when it feels like it was just yesterday when she died. Other times, it seems like decades."

Marla answered. "why did I feel that you wouldn't let us leave without asking that question? We ourselves haven't been in touch recently, but from what we've heard, she is deeply involved in helping recent arrivals to adjust. We do, however, know for a fact, that she keeps an eye on the children and that she's been around you quite often during your tough times. Again, you'll probably find out much more later."

It got quiet for a while. Ever since Mardai died we've remembered her every day. It's not like being unwilling to let go, but more of a feeling that there is just a thin veil that separated her reality from ours. During quiet moments, the veil splits for a while and there is contact between the two worlds—hers and ours. I really feel it so strongly at times. I can almost hear the voices of those who have moved away from us into that other world.

"Not different realities, John," said Gideon, breaking into my thoughts, "one reality with different perspectives and interpretations and aspects."

"Gideon, I guess it's about time for us to leave," said Marla.

Gideon nodded and said, "We'll be in touch with you again soon, John. We'll also tell you a little more about the greatest secret of life. Don't worry, we'll pop in from time to time."

Marla stood up, walked around the table, held my hand, squeezed it very gently and said, "Don't look so sad, dear John. Life is meant to be a journey in joy, a major celebration. You'll see." She leaned over, gave me a hug and both she and Gideon went out the door waving good-bye as they left.

I sat there alone for a while, wondering about these two other-worldly friends of mine who have come into my life on a number of occasions to teach me the secrets of the universe. Now they tell me that there is actually only *one* secret and they'll help me find it. I was ready.

Chapter Four

The Birds and the Books

Early one morning, I was sitting at my kitchen table gazing out the window at nothing in particular. For me, this is a wonderful time of day. In it, I prepare myself for whatever the day may bring and at the same time, try to bring some unique gifts to the day.

My office is now in my home so the commute from home to office takes less than thirty seconds by foot. Instead of finishing breakfast and going directly to my office, I spent some time enjoying the view from the window. Since we were up late the previous night and there was no school scheduled for today, the children were sleeping in.

Normally, outdoors on a day such as this, there are two or three blue jays, a cardinal or two, a couple of squirrels and a chipmunk. They come to feed on the seeds we leave for them and their social habits made it possible for them to tolerate one another in such a way that each one gets his fair share of seeds. While witnessing their antics I noticed several blue jays appear nearby. Moments later, a number of cardinals joined the group followed by a few robins and some little yellow finches.

So many years I've lived in this house and watched the birds in the early morning hours, but never have I seen so many different species at one time at the feeder. I became increasingly more curious as the entire area surrounding the tree began to fill up with a variety of birds and animals. There were now a couple of rabbits—I knew that we'd spotted a few of those. Some squirrels joined the congregation and two more chipmunks arrived on the scene.

All in all, it appeared like an animal jamboree. The multicolored feathers of my flying friends blended with the colors of the small animals, leaves and trees creating an animated painting-in- motion. This vision drew me back in memory to a dream I experienced when I was barely seven years old. All through my travels and the intervening years, I've always held vivid memories of this dream, but could never make much sense of it.

It was early morning in the dream and I was sitting under a large tree near my family's farm. It was a mango tree, one of those magnificent old giants native to the coastal regions of Guyana. It was the season when its leaves shimmered in multi-colors of gold, purple, green and orange. A soft breeze was blowing through the leaves and there was a peace that far surpassed anything I've ever known.

On the ground next to me under the mango tree was a blue book with beautiful, gold lettering printed on its cover. I picked it up and tried to read the title, but I couldn't understand it because it was written in a strange language. I opened it, turning to the first chapter whose title, much to my surprise, was written in English. It read, "The Beginning." The rest of the pages were blank until I came to about the middle of the book where there was what seemed to be a line written in the same strange characters as the title of the book.

Somehow, even as a little boy, I knew I was dreaming and I knew that this dream was meant to be remembered. I kept turning the pages until I came to the last one. There, in beautiful script penmanship, were the words, "Another Beginning" and under those words, as if in a sub-title, another line which read, "No Endings, Just Beginnings."

I turned back to the middle of the book and again stared at the strange characters. I wanted desperately to know its meaning. Slowly I closed the book and replaced it where I'd first found it. The dream continued. I turned around and looked toward the woods that bordered the farm and beheld a most amazing sight. Amid the sounds of rushing air, somewhat like the winds onshore when a storm approaches, and from all directions hundreds of brilliantly plumed birds in flight were headed toward my tree.

I sat there in a state of blessed bewilderment as they landed, converging all around me. Some alighted on the branches of the mango tree and others landed next to me on the ground. Most were tropical birds although some were species I had never seen. There were kiskadees and blue sackis, red-billed toucans and spur wings, blue gauldings and scarlet ibis. The strangest part of this incredible scene was that each bird carried a tiny book in its beak. The books seemed to be miniature replicas of the one that I had opened, which now lay beside me.

As if on cue, each bird grabbed its book in one foot, opened it with its beak and started to sing in its own peculiar way. Melodies streamed into the early morning air and for a moment, it was like being surrounded by an enormous, well conducted symphony orchestra. It was like listening to celestial music of such beauty and magnitude that to this very day, I've never heard anything so sublime.

Then the singing stopped and each bird brought his little book, placed it in a pile next to my big book and flew off. And thus the dream ended. I awoke immediately and remained awake for the rest of the night enjoying countless replays of my dream. There was a feeling of great peace and joy, a fantastic feeling that comes only on a handful of occasions during a lifetime.

Throughout the years, I've told a number of people about this dream and most times, they look at me, shake their heads and smile while muttering something incoherent. Yet, it's the only dream I've remembered so precisely from childhood—the birds, their books, their brilliant colors and the music. Every once in a while, I'd still wonder what message was hidden in that strange language and would reflect on its meaning, if indeed there was any meaning.

And so, the scene outside my window triggered old memories of my childhood dream. Such strong similarities are never coincidental. Actually, nothing is ever by coincidence, but is tied by invisible strings that run across time and space to events in other places and times. As I looked at the birds gathered in the back yard around the huge oak tree, my wandering imagination may have taken over for I swore I saw a book lying under the tree.

It must be my imagination I thought, as I squinted, refocusing and, yet, it seemed so real. Reality can be different in different states of awareness. A good quantum physicist or credible scholar of philosophy would confirm that the reality experienced in dreamtime is as real to the dreamer as the reality one experiences during waking hours. To change reality from the dreamtime, all one has to do is wake up. Perhaps, for us to experience reality as it really is, we might have to wake up from being awake.

Real or not, it did appear that a book was lying under the oak tree. By this time, the birds had finished their singing and were dispersing. They were getting ready, as humans do, to face the newborn day. A few seconds later, curiosity grabbed me by the collar and led me outside, down the steps to where the oak tree stood next to the bird feeder. I reached for what I thought was the book, reminiscent of the one in my dream, only to discover it was a blue sheet of paper, probably blown there by the stormy winds of the night before.

I was about to crumple it and toss it in the garbage when I noticed some lettering on one side. I looked more carefully, squinting, since I wasn't wearing my reading glasses. To my surprise, the words, "No Endings" were written in gold in the most beautiful script handwriting. Instinctively, I flipped the sheet over, looked on the other side, and beheld the same handwriting with the inscription, "No Beginnings."

Surely, a neighbor must have been playing a board game with the family and a piece of paper blew out of their house, through the screen door and came to rest under my tree with the very words I had seen in a book in a dream when I was seven years old. No explanation made sense at this time. Since I'd learned long ago that not everything makes sense immediately, or sometimes ever, I went back into the house and sat for a while, attempting to analyze this strange incident.

A phone call interrupted my reverie. It was Gideon asking if I'd had an interesting morning. I blurted out the incident of the birds and the books and the paper and the music and whatever else I could recall. I commented how curious it seemed that dreams of yesteryear could leap across the crevices of time onto the pages of today.

"When you think about it, John," he said, "there really is no past nor future, no beginnings nor endings, just the ones that we create in our minds depending on our current perspective. A thousand lifetimes in a million years or a million lifetimes in a thousand years, what does it matte, anyway? We've always been alive."

"Doesn't it get lonesome being the only one with all the answers, Gideon?" I taunted. "And I'm sorry, why did you say you called?"

"I didn't say, but since you asked," he said, "no special reason. Just wanted to tell you it's not the answers that we have problems with. We have all the answers. What we need are the questions... ."

"What did you say about no beginnings or endings just a few moments ago?" I interrupted.

"Words are just symbols of meaning and not the meaning itself. They are not the best representatives of truth, but in their own way, they do express it somewhat. In other words, don't confuse the map with the territory. By the way, still interested in going on that trip?"

"What and when do I pack?" I asked.

"You don't have to pack anything. A good part of the trip is internal," he said. "And as to when? The answer is when it's most appropriate."

"Actually, where are we going, Gideon? And what are we searching for?" I asked.

"You are searching for the *one* secret of life, John. The one that was written in the middle of the book you found beneath the mango tree when you were seven years old. The secret you couldn't read because you didn't understand the language."

"So you knew about that, eh Gideon? Was that really the secret of life written there? There were just a few words. Is that all there is to it? A simple little secret?"

"Simple. Not easy," he replied.

"Do you think we'll ever find it?" I asked.

"It's not the finding that's difficult," he replied, "it's the recognizing."

"Well, I'm looking forward to all this," was all I could say.

"Not to worry, John," he replied in that tone which always brought me a sense of assurance and comfort. "We'll take care of all that. And of course, Marla will be there, too." There was a pause, then he added, "That's all for now. You'll hear from us soon. Bye." The phone went dead.

The day hadn't really started and already it seemed like I'd been awake for many hours. The children must be awake, I thought, because I could now hear footsteps coming downstairs. Malika came into the kitchen, said good morning and casually mentioned a weird dream about birds that read books. But she couldn't remember any details. Interesting, I thought... very interesting.

Chapter Five

Return to Tomorrow

My father once told me the story of the Ambrose Stone. He never mentioned from where it got its name, but said that it was a stone infused with miraculous power. If you touched a sick person with it, that person would be healed. If you slept with it under your pillow, you would have dreams of the future and would be more able to plan your life in a way that would be most beneficial.

The Ambrose Stone, my dad said, would bring its owner, love, joy, peace, health and prosperity. Naturally, I asked him where the Stone could be found. Unfortunately, he sadly replied that he did not know and told me he had heard the story from the old man who lived by the river. At that time I was just a young boy and, much as I wanted the Stone for my own gratification, I didn't know where to begin searching.

This, of course, did not prevent me from pestering Dad with all sorts of questions about the possibility of finding and using the Stone. I thought of all the things I could do, all the people I could heal, all the magic I could perform. Well, not really. Being a little boy, I thought only of selfish things. I even announced to my dad that I'd use the power of the Ambrose Stone to wreak revenge on the neighborhood bully. At that, my dad smiled sadly and motioned me to come closer. I was only eight or nine years old at the time, but I still remember his voice as he passed his hand through my hair and said, "Listen carefully to what I will tell you now, son."

"Tell me, Dad, tell me," I fairly squirmed with glee. Surely he must have discovered the location of the Ambrose Stone.

"You will only find this Stone when you have grown in understanding and love. And then you will not need it because the power of the Stone is not where you think it is."

How could anyone expect a small boy to understand such things? Gone forever was my glorious chance, my delicious moment of revenge on the bully. During the following week a stranger came through the village. Strangers rarely came this way so, many of the villagers wanted to know why he was here. Some said that he was a holy man and should be treated with the utmost respect. Others thought him to be a vagrant and wished he'd leave as soon as possible.

The stranger was dressed more as a wandering minstrel than one who was gainfully employed. He said he wouldn't be staying long—just wanted to rest for a little while before going on a long journey. Word went around that he was looking for a place to have a meal.

My mother, perhaps one of the kindest souls I've ever encountered, hearing of the stranger's need, sent me to invite him for a meal. Though times were tough, there always seemed to be enough for an extra mouth at our table. Half-scared, yet somewhat excited for having an opportunity to speak to him, I rushed down the lane. I found him standing alone in the shade of a neem tree and walked up to him. Perhaps, this traveler knew where I could find the elusive Ambrose Stone.

I told him that he was welcome to join us for dinner. He looked at me with a long, piercing gaze, then finally smiled. He had the gentlest, most peaceful voice as he said he didn't want to be any trouble. I assured him that there was no problem and that my mother insisted that he come. He accepted and then, as an afterthought it seemed, he winked at me and asked, "Now tell me, little one, are you still looking for that stone?"

After the initial shock at his knowing my thoughts, I said, "Yes, sir. The Ambrose Stone. Do you know anything about it?"

"Just some old stories," he replied, "But I have no idea where it is."

He followed me home where my mother served dinner and my father carried on a lengthy chat with him. He said he was a traveler and that he was on a journey to meet an old friend. He seemed not to want to comment any further on the details of his life. How exciting to have this gypsy adventurer visiting my home! I was spilling over with questions, but it would have been considered extremely impolite to bother a guest.

After dinner was finished, he thanked us and said that he must be on his way. We asked him to stay a while longer, but he insisted he had promises to keep and a long journey ahead. As he was about to leave, he hesitated and turned to face us once more. Putting his hand in his pocket, he pulled out a small pouch and handed it to me.

In my family it was customary never to accept payment for any good deed we did for others, so I said, "No thank you, sir."

"Oh no! This isn't money... of that, I have very little. I don't have the Ambrose Stone either, but this is another stone called the Jahar-Mora. If you're ever bitten by a snake or stung by a poisonous insect, hold the Jahar-Mora to the wound and in five to ten minutes, it will draw the poison out and you'll be fine. It will also bring you good fortune." Waving good-bye, he departed; I never saw him again.

I kept the stone in a little box with the few other "treasures" I'd collected, then promptly forgot about it until one day, walking through the woods, I accidentally disturbed the nest of some ill-tempered, South American wasps. Before I knew it, there was a sharp sting over my right eye and stunned, I fell to the ground. The pain was so terrible that I could hardly get up, but finally I was able to stumble back home. By this time my eye was almost swollen shut and I was beginning to run a high fever. The sting from this type of wasp could make you very ill. Some children were known to have died from it. I was really scared.

My parents were visiting neighbors so, I fumbled to open my special box and reached in for the little pouch containing the Jahar-Mora. I pulled out the stone and, with a tremendous strain, tried focusing on it with my uninjured eye. It was a strange color and felt surprisingly cool to the touch. Slowly I raised it to my face, pressing it against the swollen lump, and held it there. At first, nothing seemed to happen; but in less than a minute, the stone started becoming warm. In another minute or so, it became so hot that I had to pull it away from my face. Now it seemed to have changed to a bluish, scarlet tint.

In a short time, the pain of the sting disappeared and within ten minutes, the swelling had gone down and I was back to near normal again. I carefully replaced the stone in its pouch and gently laid it in the box. When my parents returned home, I told them about the incident and went to get my Jahar-Mora to show them how the color had changed. I reached into the box for my pouch, but it was nowhere to be found. We searched everywhere, turned the box and most of the household furniture upside down, looked in every nook and cranny, but to no avail.

My dad, in an effort to comfort me at my loss, said in a consoling tone, "Remember what I once told you? The magic is not in the stone. It's in you. You don't need the stone now. Depend on it too much and you become stone dependent. Anything you depend on too much will enslave you and control your life. Let the stone go, son. Its work with you was done. It needs to go on to its next student."

I never did find the Jahar-Mora. It was a mystery how it disappeared, but I always remembered my father's words as he said, "The magic is not in the stone; the magic is in you."

Today, I was reflecting on the Ambrose Stone and the Jahar-Mora. It was a burdensome day with many tasks to complete, financial situations to work out and numerous matters all clamoring for my attention without any solution in sight. I thought how wonderful it would be to have the Ambrose Stone. I would just put it under my pillow before going to sleep and I'd dream the solutions to all the problems that were troubling me. I would return to tomorrow, I thought, and venture back to today with answers. But the little village was decades ago and the stone... who knows?

In the middle of my contemplation, a friend called and asked if I could help with a problem she was having with her computer. I am not a computer expert and only employ them as useful tools in my work. My computer knowledge is probably more instinctive and intuitive than technical. I quickly agreed to help and before long, I was engrossed in following the paths of electrons as they danced through computer circuitry and translated themselves, byte by byte, into meaningful messages on the screen.

Working on the computer took my mind away from my problems. Breaking focus with my problems was exactly what I needed. There's an old saying that "what you focus on expands." When I was done, I felt refreshed and promised myself not to get overwhelmed by my problems for the rest of the day. At bedtime, though, I reflected again on the Ambrose Stone. What an absurd idea, I thought, everyone knows that there's no such thing as an Ambrose Stone. Crazy childhood fantasies, I thought as I drifted off to sleep.

I was up early the next morning, and quickly found myself at the kitchen table nursing a freshly brewed cup of coffee. And then I remembered. I needed to make an urgent phone call. I don't know where the thought came from, but it seemed to have been there when I woke up this morning. Though it was still early, I followed that "still, small voice" and phoned anyway.

I called an old acquaintance whom I hadn't spoken with in years, but he seemed to have been expecting my call. During our short discussion, I received some very important information, which helped me to solve some of the problems that were troubling me yesterday. This was going to be a great day!

I leaned back in my chair and smiled. It was then that I heard a voice say, "You stand at the center of your universe. You have one foot planted in yesterday and the other in tomorrow. There is no need for magic stones or strange rituals. Those are only crutches. They do work temporarily, but they're not necessary if you know what to do. You can return to tomorrow anytime you want since tomorrow and yesterday revolve around today. The music is not in the piano, the music is in you. The magic is not in the stone; the magic is in you."

I got up from the kitchen table and walked toward my office. I turned around to find the source of the voice but saw no one. Shaking my head I said, "I must be thinking out loud... too loud."

Chapter Six

The Mills of the Gods

My office is a haven where I go to concentrate while preparing for lectures, returning phone calls, answering mail from all around the world and taking care of the necessary administration of my business. My desk is the large one at the back of the room. Paintings of ships on two walls, a little shelf of angel figurines, books, clutter, all create a working environment, which harmonizes with my personality.

Computers, laser printers, scanners, copying and fax machines are lined up in one area of the office. There are a few older chairs and, of course, the insurmountable pile of paper in the corner. However, I hardly write my books here, much preferring to sit at the kitchen table.

Today, as I went into the office, I heard the sound from behind my desk... as if someone were sitting in my chair. It creaks sometimes, you see, a sound entirely unique unto itself. After the voice in the kitchen, I guess I was slightly jumpy. I quickly glanced in the direction of my desk as the grinning face of Gideon spun around in my chair, as cheerful as can be.

"Good morning," he said as he moved to a nearby guest chair. "Who did you think was talking to you in the kitchen, anyway?"

Somewhat relieved to discover it was Gideon, I sat down and mentally started to quiz him about how he got into my office without a key, when I thought better of it. He habitually appeared unexpectedly and, yet, throughout the many years I've known him, he never intruded on my privacy. He always seemed considerate of others and would never take advantage of anyone's kindness.

"So you were the disembodied voice, huh?" I muttered.

"As you can clearly see, I've got a body just like you do. I just use my mind a little more effectively. Span the universe and all that." He winked at me as he spoke.

"By the way, Gideon, what are you doing here so early in the morning? Of course, I'm always happy to see you, but just curious."

"Just a friend dropping by. Do I have to have a reason?"

"I guess, you're right," I said. "I used to think that I had quite a few friends, until I couldn't be of much use to them any longer. I thought they stayed around me because we cared about one another. But when things really got bad for me, they disappeared so fast you'd think they vanished into thin air."

"So you were mad at them because they didn't stand by you?" he asked in his best cross-examination manner.

"Well, not really. I guess I was sort of disappointed. After all, aren't friends supposed to stick with you through thick and thin?" I was thinking of how sad and lonely it was when I went through those terrible experiences of losing my business and material possessions, my wife's death, the loss of both my parents and so many other unpleasant situations. There were times I felt downright deceived, somewhat abandoned.

"Are you finished?" he asked sarcastically, as if reading my thoughts.

"Of course I'm finished," I replied.

"So when do you want it?"

"Want what?" I asked, somewhat annoyed.

"The medal. You deserve a medal, don't you?"

"What for, Gideon?" I asked, "what are you driving at?"

"You poor thing! All those friends deserting you when you needed them most! What a pity!" He shook his head in mock sympathy. He was actually laughing at me.

"That's not funny, Gideon. It's not even fair. I thought you were my friend," I said, whining in self-pity.

"Of course, I'm your friend and I'm trying to tell you that *you* can't decide how others will choose. You can only decide how *you* choose."

"I know that, Gideon. I was just reflecting on those sad times. I wished there were a few who would have stayed around. Almost all of them left."

"Then remember this, John. People leave, not because of who *you* are, but because of who *they* are. Joyce Sequichie Hifler tells of a Cherokee concept of friendship. She says, 'We talk about choosing our friends, but true friends are self-selected. It is they who decide to respond and by what method. Acquaintances wait and judge. A friend is a *unali*—without question or fear... . That is why friends are dear to us. They have chosen to be so.'"

Gideon's comment made me realize we all need to be reminded every once in a while that this is a just and orderly universe. We are safe in it and any appearances to the contrary are just that—appearances. It's the way we interpret what we observe that decides how we'll meet the situation.

"So you're reflecting on this, eh?"

"Tell me glorious, mysterious secrets of life, Gideon, not simple stuff about friendship and medals."

"Mysterious secrets?" He had a look of mock horror on his face as he continued, "You don't listen, John. I told you before, there is only *one* secret in the universe and it's extremely simple. The secret is not in the Ambrose Stone. It's not in the mountains, not in the skies or oceans. It's right within you, Johnny Boy. Yes sir! Right within you."

"O.K., O.K. So now I know where it is. Now tell me, wise guy, what is it? What's this great secret?"

"That's part of it. I can't tell you. Everyone has to discover it for himself, or else it just doesn't work."

"A just universe you say, Gideon? And yet no one to help you when you're running blind or lost? The good seem to suffer and the bad prosper. Damn it, Gideon, where the hell is justice?"

"Ha, got you going there," he said, seeming pleased that I had lost control and raised my voice.

I ignored his remark as he continued, "I'm delighted you don't seem to be 'above it all' any more. You can show some emotions and that's good. Emotions are the colors that bring variety to the picture of life. Don't control them. Manage them."

"Still doesn't seem right, Gideon," I remarked and just listened to what he had to say.

"In a way, it's not your problem, John. All your friends were given an opportunity to help and, thus, a great opportunity for growth. Those who could most afford to help you, passed up a wonderful chance for the growth of their souls. Those who could least afford, but helped anyway, gained so much in the simple act of stretching out a helping hand.

"And what do you mean by 'no one to help when you're lost or need assistance?' Well, my friend, what do you think I'm doing here? And why do you think Marla comes by? We *are* helping. Never, never forget. There is always a helping hand—*always, always, always*!

"And as to those who choose to be self-centered instead of compassionate, caring and helpful, let me repeat that ancient saying, 'The Mills of the Gods grind slowly, yet they grind exceeding small.' No angry God to punish or reward us. The system is set in such a way as to be self-balancing and self-functioning. We reward ourselves. We punish ourselves. Find the great secret and you will understand most all of these things."

"Our conversation this morning has given me quite a lot to consider, Gideon," I finally said. "Has anyone ever found this great secret?"

"Of course, John. There was Jesus. I think he demonstrated its highest use. And there were others you know such as Buddha, Mother Teresa, Mohammed, Zoroaster, Gandhi, Lincoln, Eric Butterworth and Dr. Thomas A. Dooley. Many others you've never heard of, for example: Barry Rosenbaum, Harnarine Singh, Rafael Martinez, Salvatore Bonano, Janet Jones and Marjorie Braithwaithe. And then there are some like Marla and Gideon."

"I guess, it must be worth searching for," I said.

"It's the 'Pearl of Great Price,' the most valuable thing you could ever want or hope for," he said, "it is the summum bonum of existence. And you've had glimpses of it on a number of occasions."

"I vaguely remember a few times when it seemed like I was being led by a powerful, knowing, loving force. Well, Gideon, we'll see... ."

"Marla sends her love. She says she'll see you soon. I think she really likes you. Speaks of you a lot. Hmm... . Bye, John."

Chapter Seven

Islands in the Sun

A few weeks passed since I last saw Gideon. I was busy with writing, lecturing, laundry, cooking, cleaning and all the other things that seem to make up a part of my rather typical, single parent life. Today, I thought, I'd take a break from everything. No writing this weekend. No special anything, just two days to, perhaps, catch up on my reading, enjoy some music and maybe view a movie or two. Malika was away on a trip with friends, while Jonathan was visiting relatives in another state. I miss them when they're gone, but, in a way, they were stretching their wings and I had the weekend all to myself.

I walked over to the radio and switched it on for no special reason except to hear some noise in the deafening silence of the morning. An old song from the West Indies was playing to a calypso beat. An energetic voice, spiced with Caribbean accent, belted out with rhythm and rhyme, "This is my island in the sun... " I sat quietly listening to the upbeat music until I could almost feel the trade winds blowing through my hair and the faint smell of the salt air pervaded the entire house.

It had been years since I visited those tropic isles. I can still remember many evenings, lying on the beach looking at the stars and hearing the hypnotic sound of the eternal tide, the songs of the red birds and the whispering chorus of the wind in the palm trees. It would be heavenly to be there again—if only for a day or two, I thought. How totally refreshing it would be. A rapping on the back door interrupted my daydream, as I got up to see who would be calling at this hour.

I was somewhat surprised to see Gideon and Marla this early and immediately asked them in. He was dressed in a dark, beautifully tailored business suit, blue shirt, red tie and black, well-polished shoes of the finest leather. He appeared as if he were about to attend a board of director's meeting. She wore shorts, a light, tropical cotton blouse and sandals. On her head a straw hat tilted at an angle and her long, golden hair fell in waves over her shoulders. She seemed destined for the beach. Surveying all this at a glance, I motioned them to sit.

"Well, it's great to see you both. Off on a trip, I see. But then again, you couldn't be going to or coming from the same place," I said as I gestured at their attire.

"No, I'm going to visit a friend," said Gideon. "He's experiencing some difficulties in his business and asked if I could help him get things back on track. I'll be away for a short while and then I'll join you and Marla. Would you like to hear what we have in mind?"

"Sure," I replied.

Marla took up the conversation, "We have a great idea. It's been a while since you've had a really good vacation. Every time you travel, it's been mostly for your work with hardly any time for relaxation. So we have this great idea. We're free for the next few days and I think you are, too. We thought it would be great to visit one of the 'islands in the sun.' As you can see, I'm already dressed for the occasion. What do you say?"

I hesitated for a moment, somewhat overcome by the spontaneity of their proposal. Gideon noticed my apparent discomfort and immediately jumped to the rescue. "I think it'll do you a lot of good," he said. "As a matter of fact, I think all of us could use some 'non-work.' We've all been much too busy recently. Your children are away for a while and you have the next few days all to yourself. If they need you, they could always reach you through your voice mail. You and Marla go ahead; I'll meet you both in time for dinner."

"This all sounds too fantastic," I quickly replied. "It's a great idea, but I really can't afford it—not for a while at least. Still a pile of bills to pay. But I'd love to go when funds are available."

"Don't worry about the money. It's been taken care of," said Marla.

"You mean we'll travel in one of those transdimensional shift transporters? Here one minute, there the next?"

"No, dear John, no instant travel this time," she said, "no need for that now. As they say, 'when you can walk on water, take the boat.' We'll use regular airline tickets—normal methods you're familiar with. By the way, you'll love the hotel. Right on the beach. Lots of tropical fruit and drink, calypso music to your heart's content."

"It's still going to cost a lot," I said.

"Didn't you hear me? I told you it's all been arranged. One of Gideon's friends made the weekend available. No cost—not for food, hotel, airline tickets or anything. As you know, we have connections."

"Yes, but I still feel guilty accepting such an expensive gift. You see ...."

Before I could say another word, Gideon piped in, "Why can't you just accept a gift? Why do you always make it so difficult for others to do something for you? His voice carried a slight edge of annoyance as he continued. "If you act as if you don't deserve the gifts of the universe, the universe won't be able to give you anything. Receiving is just as important as giving. If you want to receive, you must learn to give. And if you give, you must learn to receive. One cannot exist without the other."

"OK, Gideon, I get it. I'm just a bit overwhelmed at the idea of receiving such a wonderful gift—a great all-expense paid weekend. Thank you, thank you. See? I can get used to receiving very quickly."

"It's not always easy, John," said Gideon. "I have to leave now; see you both in a few hours. I'll let myself out." He turned and walked clear through the closed door, just as if it hadn't been there.

"How does he do that?" I murmured, more as an observation than expecting an answer.

"It's easy when you know how; anything is easy when you know how," Marla said.

"Yeah... sure... easy, figured you'd say that," I mumbled.

I sat silently for a while, gazing at Marla. She had appeared beautiful before, but now she was ravishing. She pretended not to notice as she browsed through a travel brochure, but I knew that she knew I was looking at her.

"Hmm...," she finally said, "if we're going, we'd better leave soon. Just three hours left before our flight leaves. I've got our tickets. Gideon's coming later."

I sprung from my chair and without further delay announced, "Give me a short while and I'll be ready." As the ad says, sometimes the best way to handle things was to 'Just do it.' I was working entirely too hard and needed a vacation badly. "My carry-on suitcase is always ready. Let me throw a few things in, find my passport and whatever and I'll be ready. 'Tis better to truly *live* one weekend than to *exist* in boredom for eternity."

"Great! I was hoping you'd come, but we've got to hurry."

Talk about motivation—with lightning speed, I was packed and ready to go. A two-day trip, whether across the ocean or a few state lines was no problem for me. I've done so many of them in the last few years that I could, so to say, pack in my sleep.

Somewhat unexpectedly a limousine arrived and in a short time we were disembarking at the airport. During check-in I was surprised to discover that our tickets were for the first-class cabin.

For so long it had been a case of 'too little, too late.' Now I was having difficulty adjusting to 'too much, too soon.'

"Way to go, John," Marla explained. "Occasionally, luxury is good for mind, body and soul. You deserve to travel first-class."

We settled into the flight and chatted quietly as we droned across the skies. Unlike the coach section, first-class seats are always comfortable and I leaned back in mine, enjoying the luxury of peace and well-being. I found the transformation from desperation mode to lap of luxury an amazingly easy one to make.

The problems of next week would have to wait until this week was done. Nothing would ruin this weekend. Lulled in comfort, I must have dozed off because the next thing I heard was Marla saying, "We should be there soon. What would you like to do when we arrive? Would you prefer to rest for a while or get involved in island life right away? It'll be a few hours before Gideon arrives."

"I'm looking forward to a wonderful weekend, Marla," I said as I stretched and yawned. "Doesn't really matter what we do. Is there anything special you have in mind?" I was somewhat embarrassed that I had fallen asleep.

"No," she said, "just doing whatever you want, would be fine with me. I've been here many times before. Remember, I can go anywhere, anywhen. But traveling this way is sometimes so much fun."

I hoped she wasn't reading my mind at this moment because I caught myself thinking of a few hedonistic things I'd really like to do. She looked up at me and smiled as if she heard my thoughts. Quietly we sat there until I leaned over and gently kissed her cheek. "Thank you," I said, "thanks to both of you for making all this possible."

"Don't mention it," she said in an almost inaudible whisper. "I think it's rather, well... let's see, special and appropriate. You deserve all good things."

Soon we were on the ground in an enchanting, tropical isle. We quickly cleared local immigration and were on our way when I heard hurried footsteps from behind and turned to see a man rushing toward us, waving his hands. "Who's that, Marla? He seems to know us," I pointed. She stopped and looked back as the man rushed up. Then she smiled a smile of recognition and said, "Oh, it's our driver. He'll take us to the hotel."

Chapter Eight

Out There Somewhere

It wasn't too long before we were riding in a colorful cab headed toward the hotel, about half an hour away. I was anxious to get to the beach and looking forward to enjoying the sun and the sea. Actually, most times at the beach, I prefer sitting under a large shady tree gazing forever at the horizon where the ocean meets the sky.

It is by the sea that I hear the whisper of the universe, the songs of the stars and the melodies in the wind. It's always good to go down to the sea again; for me it's akin to therapy. I glanced over at Marla who seemed to be relaxing with her eyes closed. Strange, I thought. We come from two totally different worlds—different perceptions, different emotions, different realities... or do we? Gideon and Marla had special license, far above the ordinary. Yet, at times, it seemed our worlds had much in common.

It was as if she heard my thoughts, for she opened her eyes and said, "Yes, we have a number of things in common with your world, but your world is my world too. In either world, yours or mine, there are very strong emotions and feelings. Can you imagine what a world would be like without emotions?"

I answered, "Perhaps less violence, more peace, less greed, more giving, less grief, more happiness...."

"And you don't think some of those things are emotions?" she asked.

"Well, in a way, but aren't some of them unhealthy emotions?"

"Healthy or unhealthy," she replied, "emotions are emotions. The river of life runs between two banks. One is the bank of prosperity, happiness, peace, pleasure and all positive things. The other is the bank of sadness, poverty, depression, grief, pain, hurts and all negative things. The problem is not that one bumps into these banks during the common voyage of life, but that one gets run aground, getting stuck on one bank or the other. Life is an ever-flowing process, which can never stop. It is connected to the sea of tranquillity, the oceans of eternity and the skies of forever. It must keep flowing. A little time on either bank is fine. However, stagnation or habit patterns develop if you spend a lifetime stuck on one bank. Remember, John, we're all on a journey in the Fields of Forever."

"Interesting," I murmured, "but I never seem to be able to figure how not to get stuck in a situation."

"You get stuck in a predicament when you're too attached to outcomes. If you worry too much about how a situation will resolve itself, if you are desperate, if you are full of fear, if you try to force your way out, you get stuck."

"So don't worry, don't try to find a solution? Is that what you're saying, Marla? How could you not be scared in the midst of turmoil? How could you not be concerned about outcomes? It's not that simple."

"It is that simple. You don't have to struggle to make things work. Create the climate in which they work, then step aside. Be calm. Follow the guidance within. No need for desperation. Fear and worry will drain your energy and make it difficult to get unstuck from a sticky situation. Let life flow. Move from fretting to letting."

"Yeah! Easy for you to say."

"Trust yourself, trust your God, trust the process."

The cabdriver tried to appear oblivious, but in reality was intent on overhearing every word we spoke. He turned around for a second and with an impish grin announced, "We almos' dere now. Anotha' couple minits, me tink. You goin' like dis place."

We grinned back and thanked him. Marla then said, "They're expecting us, so check-in shouldn't be a long procedure. Our rooms are supposed to be next to each other, yours in the middle and Gideon's and mine on either side, all with connecting balconies. That way, we could have dinner on the verandah while watching the tall ships go by."

A few minutes later found us in the lobby of a luxurious hotel, enveloped in the rhythmic beat of steel drums. As we checked in, the hotel clerk handed Marla a note. "It's from Gideon," she said, "he'll be here about five."

As our bags were being taken to our respective rooms, Marla told me that she would see Gideon and me on the balcony around dinner time in a few hours. That seemed like a good idea and would give me a chance to be alone and relax for a short while. I enjoy company tremendously but, every now and then, I have this overwhelming need for solitude— no crowds, no chatty friends, no anybody, just I my God and myself.

The room was more a suite than a regular hotel room and the views of the beach and the ocean were spectacular. No crowded beaches, just one or two solitary figures walking along or propped up under a palm tree. I stood transfixed for a great while looking out the glass partition that separated me from the outside world. The scene was so peaceful and tranquilizing that my mind wandered through the gateway of memory to an episode not very dissimilar from this one.

It was a few years after Mardai's death. I busied myself trying to earn a living, raising my children and doing the necessary "daddy" things, all the while assuming the self-appointed role of 'Great Martyr.' Since her death, I'd rationalized that relationships were to be avoided at all cost. I was overwhelmed. It appeared that everything you love, you lose. I thought to myself, no one could ever approach, even remotely, the bond that Mardai and I had with each other. Perhaps, losing her was so painful that I never wanted to experience such grief again. It would be safer not to love or commit myself to another. Friends and family wondered whether I would ever get involved in another relationship.

Certainly there were some close encounters that lasted for a short time, then disappeared forever after. There was the wealthy, young maiden who felt that money was the root of all happiness. Then there was a beautiful flight attendant, followed in quick succession by a charming socialite, a women's rights activist and others. But even though we shared a number of common, non-conflicting goals, I could never achieve a level of comfort, never the feeling that I could totally be my true self. It wasn't that I didn't enjoy these relationships, but it was more like ships passing in the night—a gentle touch, then moving on.

During this period I was scheduled to attend a business conference at a luxurious location very similar to where I now found myself. My hotel room was much like this one, opening onto a balcony separated only by a panorama of glass. I had ventured out onto the balcony and draped myself over the rail, looking toward the sea. The beauty of the scene was so overpowering that I absent-mindedly started humming an old tune.

Suddenly, a voice to my right said, "Intriguing melody. What's it called?" It was the occupant of the adjoining room. I hadn't noticed her and wondered how long she'd been standing there. I stared at this smiling Aphrodite and wondered who she was and what she was doing there. "Hope you don't mind," she continued, "couldn't help overhearing—sounded lovely... somewhat makes you want to travel beyond the farthest star."

"Don't mind at all," I replied, "it's called, 'Somewhere Out There.' Written by a fellow named Henry Herbert Knibbs in his 'Songs of the Outlands.' I've always loved it."

"Oh, by the way, I'm Kimberly. My friends call me Kim," she said as an introduction.

"I am John," I replied, "good to meet you."

"Same here John," she said and as an afterthought continued, "Do you know the words to that tune, a verse or two, maybe?"

"It's more poetry than song," I said. "Here's a verse for you, if my memory serves me right."

I looked out to sea. The warm winds, the gulls' cry, the swaying palms, the distant sails of a ship and a beautiful woman made the words spring to life...

I'll dance a merry saraband from here to
drowsy Samarcand;
Along the sea, across the land, the birds are
flying south.
And you, my sweet Penelope, out there
somewhere you wait for me,
With buds of roses in your hair and kisses
in your mouth.

"Well, I've got to go now," she said, "give my regards to Knibbs. See you out there somewhere," as she waved and retreated into her room.

I stood there for a long while drinking in the sounds of the breakers as the lilting melody of "... *and you my sweet Penelope, out there somewhere you wait for me,*" carried me away.

I remembered that incident in vivid detail and replayed the tape once again in my mind as I waited for dinnertime to arrive. I glanced at my watch. Just another hour or so.

Closing my eyes, I returned to the event in my memory and hit the replay button. I remembered so well how I had left the balcony behind and had gone for a walk on the beach. Rows of oleander mixed with frangipani lined the pathways as the lingering scent of jasmine perfumed the air. Finally, I found myself under a palm tree facing the mighty ocean where each one, as in a mirror, sees himself. More of Knibbs rushed through my thoughts...

> The mountains are all hid in mist; the valley
> *is like amethyst;*
> *The poplar leaves they turn and twist; oh,*
> *silver, silver green!*
> *Out there somewhere along the sea a ship is*
> *waiting patiently,*
> *While up the beach the bubbles slip with*
> *white afloat between.*

A faint rustling made me turn as I noticed Kim walking toward me. Under the starry skies, she was the vision of an angel come to earth. The wind tossing her hair and the dancing rivers of light on the water joined in creating a vision to be envied by the gods on Mt. Olympus. "Hi, again, John," she said as she approached, "we've got to stop meeting like this, you know. Waiting for your Penelope? What else might Mr. Knibbs have to say?"

The words flowed forth with such intensity, as if Henry Herbert Knibbs himself were reciting them...

> There ain't no sweet Penelope somewhere
> *that's longing much for me,*
> *But I can smell the blundering sea and hear*
> *the rigging hum;*
> *And I can hear the whispering lips that fly*
> *before the outbound ships,*
> *And I can hear the breakers on the sand*
> *a-booming, 'Come!'*

"It touches you deep inside, doesn't it?" she said, "makes you want to just get up and go. I love poetry that speaks of the wanderlust."

"Me, too," I replied.

We stared out into the surf as she offered, "Want to join me? Just going down the beach."

"Love to," I said as we started walking. Then I asked, "Will you be staying long?"

"Another day or so. How about you?"

"A few more days then I'm gone again," I answered.

We walked for a little while then sat on the sand watching the tide come in. There are times when words are grossly inadequate to describe a moment, times when the best thing to say is nothing. It was as if the first person to utter a sound would be guilty of breaking the magical spell. So it was, as we sat there that evening hardly saying a word. Finally, it was time to return to the hotel. I got up, brushing the sand away as she stretched her arms, motioning me to pull her up.

"This evening," I quipped, "Henry Herbert Knibbs, was out there somewhere," as I drew her up, effortlessly, closer to me. She looked into my eyes, smiled and held my hand for a while. Tenderly, I moved my fingers through her golden hair, drew her face a little closer as her half-opened lips reached up to mine. And out there somewhere on a foreign strand the full moon peeked out from behind the clouds.

There are seconds when all eternity is condensed into an instant, when an instant reaches across eternity into glorious universes. There are moments whose feelings you want to freeze into emotional ice cubes, to be defrosted and savored at some future time. The kiss, passionate and tender at the same time, permeated my entire being leaving me breathless, caught between time and space in an aura of light and darkness, between two realities. Such was the mystery of this enigmatic woman who I held in my arms.

Ever so slowly she drew away until I could see her face by the dim evening lights. The wind blew a little stronger and a slight chill filled the air as I smiled at her and whispered, "That was wonderful."

We stood, arms around each other, quietly looking toward the ocean. Here again was a chance to make this moment into something more permanent. I knew I wanted to take her back to the hotel or, perhaps, just stay with her on the beach for the rest of the night. But once more, just like the other times before, I felt the urge to move on. Exquisite as the moment had been, it was only ships passing in the night.

"What are you thinking?" I asked.

"That was nice... really nice," she replied.

"Strange how things turn out, don't you think?" I said.

"Yes," she responded, and then added, "you know, every once in a while, wherever I am I'll wonder if you ever found your Penelope out there somewhere. Ships passing in the night. Good night, John. Happy journeys."

She turned and walked slowly back to the hotel. I didn't follow, but stood watching her move farther and farther away. Before disappearing over a little ridge, she looked back, threw me a kiss and was gone. I never saw her again. We hardly knew anything about each other—the type of work we did, where each other came from, what were our likes and dislikes, only that for a brief moment in time, two souls met in their journey in the Fields of Forever.

The ringing phone ended my reverie and brought me back to the present. It was Marla announcing that Gideon had arrived and we would meet in the restaurant instead of the balcony in about five minutes.

Chapter Nine

All Good Things

I pulled on my sneakers and it wasn't more than a minute before I took the elevator to the lobby. Island life is so informal that I felt totally at home. The restaurant was across the street, a short distance from the hotel. It was built in such a way that those who occupied the best seats enjoyed an unobstructed view of the ocean.

By now it was becoming dark, that strange darkness that suddenly descends in the tropics, making you think that someone had abruptly dropped a curtain between the sun and Earth. But tonight was a full moon, just like that time long ago when I was with Kimberly. It always seems to shine more brilliantly when I am away from home—a uniquely personal perception. It made me aware that I was still thinking of Kimberly as I walked into the restaurant. Gideon and Marla had already arrived and after a moment's greeting, the maitre d' escorted us to a table facing a large window. It provided us with a sweeping view of the ocean. By the pale light of the moon, the waves appeared to be dancing to the music of the wind.

"Beautiful place you chose," I said.

"Just want you to enjoy the best," replied Gideon.

"Romantic, isn't it?" said Marla.

"Especially romantic," I replied. "Actually, earlier today I was recalling a romantic situation."

"Sounds interesting," piped in Gideon, "that's an area you hardly ever discuss. I guess you always felt it was something that you could handle by yourself or too private to discuss with others. So, of course, we never brought it up. What were you thinking about, if you don't mind?"

"Oh, not much," I started to say when a waiter appeared.

"It's good to see you again, sir," the waiter addressed Gideon. "We missed you."

"I've been quite busy for the past few months, Jarvis, but I promise to visit more often."

"That's great, sir," beamed Jarvis. "When would you like dinner served, sir?"

"Oh, in about ten minutes would be fine," said Gideon, and, turning to me he continued, "I hope you don't mind, I ordered earlier so it would be ready whenever we were. I asked them to prepare your favorite dishes, John. Just a special surprise for you." Jarvis smiled and left.

"Now, John," continued Gideon, "you were telling us about a romantic situation. Was that the one with Kimberly or was it Cindy?"

I was stunned. "You knew about that? I never told anyone. It was Kimberly. I didn't think you pried into such private matters."

"Heavens! No! John, not the specifics. We do have a general idea, however, about what goes on in your life. We're still assigned to help you, you know."

"But of all the people, how did you guess it was Kimberly or Cindy? It could've been anyone else. I always knew that you and Marla know many things in ways I'm not even vaguely familiar with. But this?"

"You were wondering why you and Kim went separate ways when it was entirely possible to get to know each other better. You were broadcasting the question across the entire cosmos. People don't really read other people's minds. They pick up on the energy patterns that are sent flying all around the place."

"Never at a loss for a good explanation, eh Gideon? Anyway, I was thinking of Kim. Let me tell you how ... ."

"No need to tell me anything about it," he interrupted, "just close your eyes and see yourself in the situation for a few seconds and both Marla and I will get all the information we need to comment on the problem, if there is one."

"Yes," Marla added, "it's a much faster way of receiving information. Far better than word explanations. Words have so many different meanings and they're almost always imprecise. Try it. Close your eyes and see yourself with Kimberly."

"Weird," I mumbled, "but here goes." I closed my eyes and imagined the beach where Kimberly and I spent a few moments that evening, long ago. I was amazed at how effortless it was to recall the scene so vividly. I could see her sitting there on the beach next to me and hear her asking me about Knibbs when Gideon's voice broke in. "Here's dinner now," he said as Jarvis returned.

"It was just becoming interesting, Gideon," I laughed.

"We got the picture, John," winked Marla. "We'll get right back to it as soon as dinner's served."

Gideon knew exactly what I'd like for dinner. There were curries of various seafood like grouper and arapaima served with roti. Side dishes of chutneys, samosas and island bhajees complimented the steaming rice biryani. In the center of the table, Jarvis placed a bowl filled with succulent guavas, mangoes, sapodillas and papaya.

"Enjoy your dinner," said Jarvis as he left.

"Everything looks good," I commented, "and the coffee smells heavenly. Thank you, Gideon, this is a surprise."

"You and your coffee," remarked Gideon, "it's from the Blue Mountains of Jamaica. Now let's see," he continued as he bit into a piece of bread, "it wasn't that you didn't enjoy Kimberly's company. You certainly did and I'm sure she enjoyed yours, also. The real problem was your fear—fear of what a relationship might do to you. You value your freedom to be yourself so highly that anything that seems to threaten that freedom is quickly avoided. This is how you react to close relationship situations. It's neither good nor bad."

"So that's all there is to it? I'm just plain scared of getting close to anyone?"

"To a certain degree, John," he replied, "but it's not always quite as simple as that. You've told some of your closest associates that one of the great benefits of your work is that you have a chance to say 'good-bye' and move on. A part of you really enjoys moving on and staying free as the wind blows. Many times you are alone; rarely are you lonely. This basically has been your choice."

"What we're trying to tell you, John," added Marla, "is that it's OK to have a relationship. It's also OK not to have a relationship. Either or neither is fine. A relationship between two people is really about you and not the other person. Relationships, committed or non-committed, meaningful or meaningless, just reflect who you are. Enjoy your relationships; don't analyze them to death. Even fleeting ones, such as with Kimberly, create excitement."

After a brief pause, I looked up at Marla and asked "have you ever had a serious relationship, a significant other? Or do you, Gideon and others like you have no need for intimate relationships? Tell me, do you love as we do?"

At first she giggled, but her efforts to remain straight-faced resulted in a coughing fit. Rather than showing concern, Gideon broke into hysterical laughter. Marla joined until tears were streaming down both their faces.

Gasping for breath Gideon exclaimed, "Tell him, Marla, tell him about the time you gave up your job for the stockbroker in the Big City. Or, how about the time you almost ran away with the wandering minstrel."

"No, no," she protested, "you tell us about the peasant's daughter who lived by the banks of the Yangtze Kiang. Tell us how you wanted to forsake lifetimes of learning just to be her love? Or the Greek princess you met on that cruise in the South China seas. Remember, Gideon? You wanted to take a leave of absence. It took you quite a while to get over that one."

"What! You have to deal with this stuff, too? I thought you were well beyond such mortal emotions. I can't imagine Marla settling down, raising a family and embracing domestic life. And Gideon," I continued in mock horror, "I certainly can't picture you attending little league games or dance recitals."

"We're really not all that different from you, John," he replied, "we're affected by the same emotions as you are. We are as human as you are and as divine as you are, for we all came from the same source. We are all created in the Image of the Infinite. We are what you are becoming."

"The difference," added Marla, "is that we have learned how to manage our emotions instead of letting them control us. Oh yes, every once in a while we get off track, but who doesn't? Also we're more prone to seek the guidance which is always there—to ask for help when we're confused. You can do the same. Ask, seek, knock. There is help available all the time. Plug in to the source. You should have seen Gideon when he wanted to marry the Greek princess. He was prepared to leave G & M Enterprises, give up all his benefits for the love of a woman."

"And, you wouldn't have believed that Marla was willing to forgo all she held dear to spend a lifetime with an itinerant musician. You should have seen her then. Willing to give up everything for the love of a man."

"So, was that wrong?" I asked. "Don't you both deserve happiness in whatever way you choose?"

"Of course, it wasn't wrong," replied Gideon, "it's not a matter of right or wrong. It rarely is. It was just that I was caught up with the seeming pleasures of the moment and thought they would last forever. I nearly forgot my mission and why I was here. The same is true for Marla. We discussed the situation and our feelings at length. The Chief helped us each time. We've grown through those experiences and I rather suspect that there will be other, similar ones."

"Isn't it a pity that all good things must come to an end?" I asked. "My life with Mardai, for example, vanished into thin air, family and friends disappeared; new relationships developed as old ones faded away. A Kimberly appears for an evening, a dynamo of energy, passion and joy. Here this moment, gone the next and all good things come to an end."

"Law of change, John," said Gideon, "all growth consists of change. No change, no growth, only stagnation. Everything comes to pass. And No! All good things do not have to come to an end. All good things can get better. Where there's a 'good' there's a 'better' and where there's a 'better' there's a 'best.' All good things continue *only if they change*. You'll know this when you discover the one great secret of the universe."

After a slight pause, Gideon took a sip of his coffee and continued, "Life is forever. It flows through time and space, sometimes slowly, other times much faster depending upon your perception of time. It's a journey, not a destination. Life is not the candle nor the flame. *It's the burning.*"

"And there will be others like Kimberly, other times and places of adventure and hope," Marla added. "You'll meet parts of your soul everywhere you go. And every bend in the river is an indication that life is forever flowing."

As I sat with these two special friends, I still found it hard to believe that even souls so advanced as they are still faced with emotional choices—eternal pains and pleasures of life. The journey never ends.

As we leisurely strolled back to the hotel, the echo of the rhythmic waves crashing against the island crags sent forth a healing stream into the rivers of my mind. Yes, all good things... .

Chapter Ten

"Unto Everything, There is a Season and a Time..."

The three of us spent the next day enjoying the music of calypso bands and sitting on the beach. The sun was disappearing over the horizon and evening was not far off so, I walked over to a cluster of coconut trees. This was a paradise custom-made for daydreaming and I took full advantage. I daydreamed of roaming the world, dropping by to see the fjords of Norway while enjoying the Land of the Midnight Sun, walking by the Hanging Gardens of Babylon or sailing down the Potaro River to see the mighty Kaieteur Falls of Guyana.

I probably would have drifted off, had it not been for the thought that there were not many hours remaining and soon we'd be flying back home. The few people on the beach had already gone. Since only the three of us remained, Gideon and Marla came and stayed with me under the coconut palms for a while. Only the three of us remained. "In a few hours we must leave," said Gideon, stating the obvious.

"I guess, back to the real world soon... right?" I muttered.

"This is the real world, John," replied Marla, "wherever you are is the real world. Some folks would call this an illusion instead of reality. What does it really matter? A rose by any other name... ."

Gideon stood up and announced, "I'll go ahead. See you both in an hour."

"We'll be there," said Marla as Gideon brushed some sand from his arms and proceeded back to the hotel.

"Don't feel like leaving yet, Marla," I said.

"We still have a little while so, no rush," she replied.

"You know, Marla," I said as I turned to face her, "I can't believe you were involved with a stockbroker and a musician."

"Why?" she asked, "do you think I'm incapable of emotional involvements?"

"No, not incapable," I replied, "maybe just above those feelings. Perhaps, somewhat distant, managing to keep emotions at arm's length. Even more surprising, what were you doing cohorting with mere mortals?"

"Well, you and I are similar in some respects, then," she replied in a rather clipped tone.

"What do you mean?" I asked.

"Haven't you noticed that there are a number of friends and associates who think you are above those feelings too? Don't you seem distant to those who would really want to get closer to you?" She had a way of answering questions with more questions.

"I'm not above them," I protested. "I can hurt as terribly as the next person, soar to heights of ecstasy, descend to depths of despair. I can be as happy or as miserable as anyone."

"Well, so can I, John," she replied, "so can I. And as to being with mere mortals, I'm here with you right now. Aren't you a mere mortal? If this is your line of reasoning, what am I doing here with you?"

For a moment I was taken aback. I never looked on myself as a mere mortal. I always thought that there was more to every living being on earth, more than we realized. "No, Marla," I objected, "I am not just a mortal. I'm a citizen of the universe, a child of the Infinite. I am as valid as you and Gideon are. I may, at this moment, inhabit a mortal body but my spirit is free to roam the cosmos."

"Then you've answered your own questions, John," Marla replied with a mischievous, subtle smile. "The stockbroker and the musician were not just 'mere mortals.' They were as we are. And yes, I have emotions and, like you, I have problems dealing with them sometimes. We—you, I, Gideon and all others came from the same Source. Sure, we're unique, but we have much more in common than we have differences. And the differences are actually those of awareness. Your degree of enlightenment is directly proportional to your degree of awareness of who you are. Naturally, an open, curious mind is a prerequisite."

"But, Marla," I persisted, "if you were in love with a wandering troubadour, there must have been something about him that was extremely attractive. Was he tall, dark, handsome? And the stockbroker? Was he the head of his firm? Was he rich? You and Gideon never seem to be in want of material things. I mean, c'mon Marla, what attracted you to them?"

"If you're referring to their physical qualities, John, that wasn't the reason. Physical attributes change. A beauty today may not be a beauty tomorrow. There is something much more important than physical characteristics. It's something of the spirit. Coming from deep within, its expression overshadows everything else. It's an attraction of the soul, that invisible part of you that has always been and always will be. That's how it was with Peter, the stockbroker and Carlos, the minstrel. Their spirits radiated light to such an extent that I was drawn to the beauty of their souls." Marla became quite still for a few moments as we sat there, side by side, looking out to sea.

To break the silence, I said, "I see. You bring into your experience, those who are similar to you. Then there is the matter of choices. There was nothing wrong with your wanting to be with them. Then why then did you give it all up?"

She leaned toward me and answered in a voice so soft that it was almost a whisper. "It was a situation of... let's see... 'Ships passing in the night.' Somewhat similar to you and Kimberly. I should have known that it was time to move on. For some of us there is one relationship that lasts an eternity. For others, relationships may last for only a short while. Each makes a choice. Each chooses his or her own destiny. I had to go on. I had work to do and worlds to see."

"I guess it's like everything else," I said. "Too focused and too much of a narrow view and you're in trouble. Not focused at all, with desires running all over the place, you're still in trouble. The old 'moderation in all things,' or the need for balance, right?"

"To a certain degree, yes," she answered. "But there are other factors involved. As we learn the one secret of the universe we begin to find ourselves and, in doing so, we begin to understand, accept and live happier, more fulfilled lives."

"Every once in a while though, don't you think of Carlos or Peter? Don't you miss them or wonder how your life would've been had you decided to stay with them?"

She quickly shot back, "Do you think of Kimberly every once in a while? And do you wonder what it would have been like if the two of you had decided to pursue a relationship?"

"Yes, I do. But those thoughts don't occupy every waking moment. Now and then I'll close my eyes and see her on that beach. Sometimes the vision is so strong and clear that I can almost sense her in my arms and feel her lips against mine. There was that electric spark from the moment we met. I guess it happens all the time." I looked at my watch and saw that the time for leaving had arrived.

"When we examine others' choices, we sometimes see a reflection of our own," she said as she started to get up. "Time to be on our way."

"It's been a great weekend, Marla," I replied, and as I stood up, she lifted her arms for me to help her up. I took them and slowly pulled her into my arms. It was almost dark and flashing before me was the picture of Kimberly. I held Marla close and ran my fingers through her hair. She smiled and suddenly, without even meaning to, I gently drew her face to mine and kissed her softly on the lips. Her lips parted and for a lingering moment, we stood there, enveloped in a blinding flash of joy.

"There!" she said as she slowly drew away, "that was fantastic. Where did you learn to do that?"

I knew that she wasn't upset by what happened. In fact, I felt she knew it would. "Didn't really mean to, Marla," I said, "I just got carried away."

"Don't be silly, John. That was marvelous. Right time, right place, right feelings. A time and place for everything, you know." She hesitated a second then added, "You seem somewhat upset. I thought you enjoyed it, too? What's the matter?"

"Of course, I liked it. But it's just that you're, well... you know... it's that you are... "

She interrupted, "It's just that *I am Marla*, right?"

"That's it, Marla. That's just it. If you were an ..."

Again she finished my thought, "... an ordinary person. You were about to say that if I were an ordinary person, it would have been fine." She took my hand and started walking back to the hotel. "If I were someone you felt comfortable with at all levels, you would have thought it was all right. Correct?"

"In a way you're right, Marla. You are such a special person. You seem to have superhuman abilities. You're so beautiful, so profound and so understanding. I just felt that you were out of my reach and, yet, I took a chance that you were not going to be offended."

Marla, still holding my hand, stopped, turned, looked at me and smiled. "You must learn that everyone is special and everyone is ordinary. Once there was a Guru who had mastered all the problems and challenges Earth had to offer. He could walk on water, fly at will, travel anywhere instantly and performed fantastic miracles. One day, while teaching his disciples, he became invisible for a few minutes just to illustrate a point. When he reappeared, one of his disciples asked, 'What new miracles and powers will you show us now that you have become so special?' The Guru smiled at the question and replied, 'You do not understand. The reason I can do all these things is that I have transcended. I have become ordinary.' So you see, John, the more special we are, the more ordinary we become."

"Sounds like a paradox to me," I said. "Anyway, I really enjoyed our few moments together. And don't worry. I know that 'A kiss does not a relationship make.' But goodness, Marla, that was fantastic!"

"I know," she replied, and before I figured what was happening, we were joined in another long, tender kiss. It ended only too soon. She giggled saying, "And two kisses, do not a commitment make."

We continued back to the hotel. Soon we'd be packed and ready to leave this island—this island of revelations. What reaction would Gideon have when he found out what had occurred between me and Marla?

"Gideon knows and understands much more than you could imagine. Don't analyze these things to death, John." Again, she knew what I was thinking.

"So many people hope and pray that one day, they'll meet the right partner. They go through a lifetime and still it doesn't seem to happen. Why is that Marla?"

"Simple," she replied, "don't try to meet the right person. Just be the right person and you'll see the right person as he or she comes into your reality. 'Like attracts like,' you know. It's an immutable law. Just be the best you that you can be every moment of your life. Let your true essence flow through your entire being. When the message and the messenger are one, you'll find that you have transcended; you have become so special that you're now ordinary. And, of course, you must believe that you deserve all good things. Don't be a victim of guilt. The only message guilt has for us is 'You don't deserve, you don't deserve.' Watch out for it."

By this time we had reached the hotel. I had the urge to ask Marla a very important question, but I was afraid of the answer. Yet, once more, she had the answer before I could ask the question.

"What happened back there," she said, pointing toward the beach, "was something that happened between two very good friends. It was spontaneous and the time and place were right. No guilt, no regrets. No reading anything into it. Will it happen again? In this wonderful world of infinite possibilities, who knows what could happen as we travel the road that never ends? Let's get on with life and what we must do. It's really a great adventure."

We agreed to meet in the lobby in about a half-hour for the trip to the airport. I went up to my room and as I packed my carryon, I found myself humming a tune to the haunting words of Henry Herbert Knibbs:

There ain't no sweet Penelope somewhere
that's longing much for me,
But I can smell the blundering sea and hear
the rigging hum;
And I can hear the whispering lips that fly
before the outbound ships,
And I can hear the breakers on the sand
*   a-booming, 'Come!'*

And yet, it was not a tune of sadness, but one of the joy of discovery. A part of me seemed to know without the slightest doubt that Marla enjoyed our few close moments. But at the same time, she cared enough to share some simple truths of successful relationships. Another part of me would like her to continue sharing simple truths the way she did on the beach. Perhaps, she might even progress to more complex truths. But everything in good time. The words from the book of Ecclesiastes came to my mind as I picked up my luggage and headed for the lobby:

To every thing there is a season and a time
to every purpose under the heaven:
A time to be born, and a time to die; a time
to plant, and a time to pluck up that
which is planted;
A time to weep, and a time to laugh...
A time to love and a time... .

Chapter Eleven

The Angel with the Golden Wings

The long, lazy days of summer rolled on ever so slowly into autumn. The short island vacation seemed far removed from today's reality. I hadn't seen Marla or Gideon in a while and was busy with a number of projects, working against looming deadlines. Also, there were distended piles of correspondence to deal with.

I missed Marla and Gideon and wished that there was some way to stay in touch more regularly. Even though they exhibited a degree of enlightenment beyond my comprehension and seemed to possess abilities and talents far surpassing my understanding, I had begun to think of them as just two wonderful, extraordinary friends who were totally ordinary to me. This is how it seems to work. We are a reflection of those we associate with. Run with jackals and you assume the lifestyle and thinking of jackals. Associate with lions and you will mirror their strength and grace.

Never did Marla and Gideon jump in to solve all my problems. Many times they didn't even partici- pate in the solution at all. But I knew that they were nearby cheering for me, encouraging my efforts, suggesting alternate actions and comforting me when it all seemed to fall apart, as it had done so many times in the past. They had become, perhaps, two of my closest friends.

I'd often wondered whether others were as fortunate as I to have a Gideon and Marla. Once, when I brought up the subject, Gideon assured me that each person has friends in other areas of the universe who were as close or closer than their earthly, human friends. We hadn't discussed it at length, but I had made a mental note to ask him to tell me more about this type of communication.

I do not remember taking any definite steps to find Gideon and Marla. As I recall, it was Gideon who found me and then later I was introduced to Marla. But even so, I recalled the old saying, "when the student is ready, the teacher will appear." I even went a step further, saying, "when the teacher is ready, the master will appear." I imagine we should be ready to welcome our Gideons and Marlas whenever they arrive. However, the choice is ours.

We don't have to receive them into our lives. Some individuals are afraid of such experiences. Most people are scared of what they do not understand; and when they are scared, they become angry.

In quiet times, I feel we can hear friends call to us from afar. In the everyday hustle and bustle, our chatty thoughts and the noise around us often drown their voices out. And still they call and try to help with our earthly challenges. I don't believe they ever interfere with our free will, but they do give us data to assist in our decision making process. There are times that, for our own good, they would step in and lend a helping hand.

Not only are there friends who assist us along our path, but I have also found help from some who were close to me when they were physically alive. I don't think our loved ones move on and forget all about us. I feel the bonds that existed when they were here with us are forever present and a simple thought could jump across space and time to create a direct line of communication.

It's not that the departed sit around in some ethereal office, waiting for us to call on the heavenly, open-request phone line. They certainly have lots of other things to deal with, probably much more so than they had while in the physical body. They will not interfere with our growth and learning, but I have enough reasons to believe that they find ways to lend a helping hand. If we don't feel close to them or don't want them around us, they do not bother, nor do they insist on imposing their presence.

Neither do they want us sitting around whining for help. They will help us if we ask, but they won't do our work for us, much preferring that we do all we can with what we have. They do not want us to be dependent on them, to try to live in their world before we are ready. I have felt on numerous occasions the presence of my wife. Then there are the times I could almost swear that my dad or mom or even a close relative or friend was around. It is, of course, a subjective conclusion, so I don't need to prove it to anyone. I just know that for me it is so.

Thus ran my thoughts on this beautiful, warm sunny day as I sat on my back porch contemplating the mysteries of the universe. Malika was out with a friend and Jonathan had gone to the movies. This was one of those times when you know that there's so much to do, but you find it much more enjoyable to just sit and be as lazy as possible. I call it "creative procrastination" so that my logical mind would believe I was doing something useful.

Suddenly, in the midst of my moment of leisure, the phone rang.

"Hi, John, it's been quite a while," announced the voice of Gideon.

"How are you, my friend?" I asked.

"Oh, fine, just fine. How would you like some company? We're in the neighborhood."

"It'll be great to see you again. And by 'we,' do you mean Marla is with you?"

"No, not this time. I'm with an old friend I want you to meet," he said. "We'll see you shortly."

For some reason, I was hoping it would be Marla, but I was nevertheless excited that Gideon would be stopping by for a visit. In less time than I could imagine, they arrived. With Gideon was an elegantly groomed man dressed in a dark, business suit.

Gideon introduced us by saying, "John, I'd like you to meet a dear, old friend of mine. This is Matthias. Matthias, meet John."

"Hi, Matthias," I said, shaking his hand, "it's good to meet you. Would you like to come inside or should we relax here on the porch?"

"The porch is fine with me, John," said Matthias as he and Gideon seated themselves on deck chairs. "Gideon told me that you get many of your creative ideas while sitting back here."

"Ah, he told you that, did he? And what else has he been telling you?" I laughed.

"Just a little of this and some of that," he replied with a teasing smile.

"And how do you two know each other, Matthias? I thought Gideon had very few friends," I kidded.

"He has friends all over the cosmos," Matthias replied. "He and I have had quite some adventures together. We go way back. It's a long story."

Gideon laughed and announced in a matter-of-fact manner, as if he were telling me about the weather, "Matthias is what you'd call an angel, John. He's on a short visit here..."

"An angel? You're an angel, Matthias?" I asked in disbelief.

"Oh yes," he said, "I've always been an angel. I'm sure you've met others like us. It's great when assignments bring me this way. I don't get to see Gideon and Marla too often."

"You know Marla, too?"

"Who doesn't?" he replied.

"But you aren't dressed like an angel," I said.

"They call him," said Gideon, "the Angel with the Golden Wings. Show him your golden wings, Matthias."

I knew they were enjoying seeing me so confused. As I watched, Matthias pulled up his left sleeve to reveal a bracelet. On the bracelet was a charm—a pair of little gold wings, the kind you might find at any good jewelry store. "These are my golden wings, John, a left-over from the old days when everyone expected us to have large feathery wings that flapped as we flew. It was quite a dumb idea because the stupid things would go unstable at high speed and, had it not been for our celestial flight mechanisms, you'd literally have seen many falling angels. But what can I say? The people expected us to have wings, so wings we had. Now I carry my wings on this bracelet as a reminder that if the Chief wanted me to have birds' wings, He would have made me a bird."

"He means every word of it John," said Gideon.

"You better believe it," continued Matthias. "Now we are permitted to dress whatever way we see fit—mostly to fit the assignment. Once I got my wings caught in a clump of trees. You should have heard me swear. You think I can't swear, huh? Well, I've been to all kinds of places and met all sorts of people. I've learned their languages well. You should hear me swear in Bantu. You've got to be good with languages, you know—part of the requirement for getting into angel school."

"Angel school?" I was surprised. "I didn't know you guys had to go to school."

"Doesn't everybody go to school? If you want to qualify for whatever you do, you've got to go into training or to some sort of apprentice program. Yep! Angel Academy. That's where we all 'earn our wings,' ha! Ha! Ha! Couldn't help that."

"Hope you're not auditioning for stand-up comedian while you're here. Don't give up your day job," I countered.

Gideon noticed that I was beginning to wonder whether I should take Matthias seriously, so he said, "Matthias actually holds a very important position within the hierarchy, John. He does have an outlandish sense of humor which, I imagine, even you wouldn't appreciate, but there again, it's kept him sane all these eons. He's on a journey now to the Big City. Thought he'd drop by and see me. He'll see

Marla at Headquarters in the Big City. Remember G
& M Enterprises? World Headquarters in the Big
City?"

"Certainly, I remember your Headquarters. So
that's where Marla is. Will you be staying in the City
for a while, Matthias?"

"No, not this time, John," responded Matthias,
"very sad case is taking me there. A little girl, Earth
years—approximately nine or so. Her dad died a few
years ago and her mom is an alcoholic. Every few
months the mother gets a new boyfriend. Although
it wasn't the most pleasant of environments,
Christine, that's the little girl's name, has always
been strong and courageous. But her mom married
the latest boyfriend. Now he beats both mother and
child and, on a number of occasions, has threatened
to burn them alive in their own apartment. That's
the case I'm working on." His voice trailed off as if
he could feel the little girl's pain.

"Isn't there anything you can do?" I asked.

"Oh, sure. But I've got to be careful. Lots of rules
about interference, free will, choices and the like.
Much as I'd rather hang the stepfather by his toes
from the tallest steeple, my job is really to

strengthen, comfort and teach Christine. I also want to assure her that the situation is temporary."

"How did you hear about her, Matthias?"

"She prayed. She prayed so fervently and honestly that the response was instantaneous. We monitor all sincere requests. Help is available immediately for those who know how to pray."

"Are you her Guardian Angel?"

"No, I'm not. Her Guardian Angel asked for my expertise; that's how I ended up with this assignment. Sometimes a Guardian Angel acts as a general manager and calls in experts from various areas. I'll be through with this case in a short while and, if conditions permit, I'll drop by and visit with you and Gideon on my way back."

"What are you going to do for Christine, Matthias?" I asked, fascinated that he was an angel.

"We're making arrangements to get her away from her stepfather. We are also in the process of helping her mother develop more confidence and find a better job. This will take a little time so, I'm giving Christine a gift, which will assist her whenever the stepfather becomes overly abusive. Here, want to see?" He opened his briefcase and pulled out a small pouch. He handed it to me and said, "It's a small gift. A stone. She will believe that it has magical powers and, because beliefs can be so powerful, she will be protected from her stepfather—at least to a certain extent. Take a look at the stone."

For some strange reason the pouch seemed familiar. I opened it and removed a small, grayish stone that felt cool to the touch. My mind jumped across the years as I remembered the day an old man had given me a similar pouch with a stone called the *Jahar-Mora*.

I held the stone in my hand for a few moments, then said, "This stone, Matthias, it looks and feels like..."

I didn't finish the sentence. Gideon did that for me by asking, "... feels like the Jahar-Mora from your boyhood days?"

"Yes, yes," I stammered, "mine disappeared forever, shortly after it was used."

Matthias looked at me with a kind smile, "I know. When I gave it to you, it was only for a short..."

"You gave it to me?" I exclaimed, "you were the old man I met in the village? How... what do you mean?"

I was almost speechless. Matthias, got up and came over to me. He slapped me on the back and said, "Yes, John. I was that old man in your village. Don't you know angels can be anything they want to be? You and your family were so kind to me and you didn't even know that I was an angel. It's a good policy to be kind to strangers because you never know exactly whom you'd meet. Actually, it doesn't hurt to be kind to everybody."

"But after I had used the stone, it disappeared and I never found it again," I complained.

"Its work with you was done. Some other little boy or girl needed it. We have many of them. The power isn't really in the stone, you know. But I must go now," he said. "I have to help Christine before her stepfather returns and beats the hell out of her."

"I'll see you soon, John," said Gideon as he, too, got up. "I think I'll visit the Big City with Matthias. Go to Headquarters and all that."

"Catch up with you soon," said Matthias. "An angel's work is never done."

They said good-bye and waved as they walked away. Then Matthias stopped and turned around. "I think I'll give her the golden wings instead of the Jahar-Mora," he said, "Stones are for little village boys. Jewelry for big city girls. No difference, however, they both work just as well once you believe."

Chapter Twelve

The Jewel in the Crown

It would be weeks before I'd see Gideon again. My heart went out to little Christina and my greatest hope was that Matthias would be able to help her. Then again, wasn't he an angel and didn't angels have magical powers? And angel or human, wouldn't he have compassion on a child? Children are God's greatest gifts to this world. Long after we are gone, they remain, trying to clean up the messes we've left behind. At the same time, they try to improve upon the good things we contributed.

It is a strange, mystical, ordinary, wonderful, miserable, fantastic life that I live. If that statement seems paradoxical, then so be it, for that is the stuff life is made of. Our paths are not always strewn with flowers and the sun doesn't always shine on our efforts. There are times when the road becomes rocky and the wind chills our very bones. During those rough times, it's no use to whine. There are already too many "whine"-a-holics around. At times, it feels as if they have all decided, coincidentally, to pay me a visit. It's not that I haven't whined; it's just that whining is a way of finding excuses, blaming others, playing a victim or just playing host to a pity party. Whining gets us nowhere fast. It drains what energy we have and creates a self-fulfilling whirlpool of negativity that sucks everything down into its perilous depths.

People like to be around others who make them feel better about themselves. Too much of a self-centered attitude drives others away. Perhaps, the secret lies in helping others to achieve happiness. And speaking of secrets, I've been hoping that Gideon and Marla would tell me more about this "Greatest Secret in the Universe." They've alluded to it so many times in their conversations that I'm prepared to tell them to forget it if they have no intention of telling me what it's all about.

And so, my mind ran from one topic to another as I packed for an upcoming trip. My work sometimes takes me overseas, to different cultures, peoples and places. This time, business was taking me to the land of my ancestors, a land of contradictions, the mysterious sub-continent of India. It would not be my first visit to that country.

I'd been there before, as both my children were adopted in India—Malika first, followed by Jonathan a few years later.

I had the opportunity, in my earlier visits, to experience the extremes and subtleties of this paradox known as India. Opulence and wealth existed side by side with poverty and decadence. Medieval villages, where life remained unchanged for centuries, contrasted sharply with modern, urban metropolises. Holy men dressed in long, flowing robes shared the crowded streets with executives in double-breasted suits or brightly colored saris. It was not strange to see a Rolls Royce jostling with a Brahma Bull for right of way through a crowded intersection. From the hustle and bustle of Bombay to the quiet waters of the Jammuna, one traversed not only time and space, but the very nature of reality. Perhaps, like everywhere, yet, nowhere else on Earth, one can find the best and the worst in India.

It would not be an extended trip, just a matter of a week, then back again. In a seemingly unending pattern there were pressing matters at home— matters like upcoming deadlines, urgent household repairs and ongoing financial crises to be dealt with, but they would have to wait until my return. I was hoping to see Gideon and Marla before I left, but it was not to be. Much as I valued their friendship and missed them when they're away, I sometimes feel that they're just a figment of my imagination and do not exist at all. But then again, how could I ever doubt the times of my knowing, the times when Gideon and Marla had shed so much light onto what seemed like hopeless, burdensome situations. No, these two have seen me through some of the worst periods of my life. I'm sure I'll be seeing them when I get back.

With the last minute details completed, I was on my way. Time seemed to ebb and flow into hours and days as airports, planes, flight attendants and taxis blended in harmony to transport one solitary traveler to his destination on the other side of the world. Day ran into night and night seemingly stretched into eternity as we droned across the oceans and continents. I must have fallen asleep a number of times before the flight ended.

Half groggy, and feeling as though I'd experienced time travel through a mix-master, I finally deplaned into the bustling airport in Bombay, searching for my good friend, Pandayji who had promised to meet me. He was always on time, this old friend of mine. We had met years earlier on my initial visit to his country. From the first moment he spoke to me, I knew we'd be friends forever. Though distance made it difficult for us to see each other more often, we have established a lively correspondence that keeps us up to date on family and business matters. It had been years since I last saw him and I so looked forward to our meeting again.

I had hardly reached the immigration and customs area when I spotted him. He had aged only slightly since the time Mardai and I waved good-bye to him at this very airport years ago. Pandayji was like the older brother Mardai never had. He treated her as if she were a princess and made absolutely certain that we would want for nothing while visiting his country. He grieved heavily when he learned of her death. His letters, expressing anguish and sorrow at my loss, brought solace to my soul and served as a balm to my spirit. This was Pandayji, my soul-brother, who greeted me now.

"You look well, my brother," he said with a trace of a tear in his eye, as he gave me a warm embrace, "it has been a long time."

"A very long time, Pandayji, but here I am again. This land seems timeless; seems like only yesterday that I saw you here."

After our initial greetings, Pandayji said, "Your visit is only a short one, so we must make the most of it. Let's clear immigration and customs and we'll go directly to your hotel. You must be exhausted."

Soon enough, we found ourselves in a cab on our way to the hotel. We spent a good deal of time catching up on personal family news. Memories flooded my mind as I checked into the hotel. It was the same one where Mardai and I had stayed when we visited India together. Even my suite was the same.

"How did you manage to arrange all this, Pandayji?" I asked.

"It was no problem, John," he replied, "for old time's sake. And, of course, I wanted you to be as comfortable as possible. You go ahead and unpack. Get some rest, if you can. We have a busy day tomorrow. I'll see you in the morning." Pandayji looked at his watch, smiled kindly and left. I knew he wanted to stay and talk, but he also knew how tired I was. That's the type of person Pandayji is.

Since it was late, I wasted no time getting ready for bed.

My suite was on the western side of the hotel overlooking the Arabian Sea. Many times, I had stood by those large, picture windows and watched the waves smash against the rocks far below. Just before turning in, I returned once more to the windows and looked over the ocean into the great void beyond. It was very dark, but there were pinpoints of light riding the ocean waves. The fishermen must be out, I thought. I was about to collapse into bed when I saw one of the lights dart across the horizon with remarkable speed.

No fisherman's boat ever moved that fast. Perhaps, it was a falling star, but this one continued to move back and forth, each time becoming even brighter. Everyone knows that meteorites do not behave in such a fashion. They glow for a short while and then are swallowed up into oblivion. By this time, an uncontrollable drowsiness overcame me and I forced myself to take the few steps to bed. I thought it must be the result of my long trip as I fell into bed forgetting lights, forgetting Pandayji and everything else.

I probably fell asleep before my head touched the pillow, but suddenly I felt totally awake and full of energy, as though I had been plugged into a revitalizing energizer. I looked around the room and was amazed to find a faint glow. Outside the picture windows was a brilliant light. The logical mind has a way of formulating theories to explain anything. It was obvious to me that I had fallen asleep and was dreaming about a bright light from a helicopter outside my window. And, of course, that was the source of the faint glow in my room. It didn't occur to me that I couldn't hear any sounds from a helicopter. But isn't that the way it is in dreams? Dreams don't have to be logical.

I was quite convinced that I was having one of those lucid dreams where you seem to be awake, yet, still dreaming. I tried to go along with the program, but still it wouldn't go away. The light outside became brighter and the faint glow in the room increased in intensity till it was almost as bright as daylight. Then, I heard voices. At first, they were faint and muffled and seemed to come from the sitting room. Now they were getting louder and clearer and I started to understand what was being said.

"He thinks he's still sleeping," said a female voice. "How are we going to get him to the meeting?"

"They are expecting him any moment now," replied a male voice. "The gathering was agreed upon. It cannot be changed now."

There was something vaguely familiar about the voices but I couldn't say where I'd heard them before. Then it struck me. They were here, Gideon and Marla. I jumped up to greet them and to tell them how glad I was that they'd come. It never occurred to me to question anything that was happening since, as far as I was concerned, this was a dream and almost anything can happen in dreams.

With one bound I was in the sitting room facing Gideon and Marla. "Hi!" I said, "what are you two doing in my dream?"

"Don't you ever get tired of asking that same question, John?" asked Marla. It wasn't as if she spoke words. And, yet, I understood all that she was saying for her voice was clear in my mind. "Remember," she continued, "no beginnings, no endings, no limitation to our friendship." She walked up to me, threw her arms around my neck and gave me a big hug. Gideon patted me on the back, then sat down cross-legged in the chair across from the coffee table.

"It must be important," I said, "for you to be in my dream. This is a dream, isn't it?"

"It's like a dream, John," said Gideon, "but not quite. You don't need words to communicate in this state. Intentions carry your meaning much more clearly than mere words. Your body is resting peacefully in bed and your consciousness is here with us. Most everyone does this, but generally they don't remember. We've done it before with you. You've only forgotten. It's a most efficient way to communicate. Some of your scientists call it out-of-body travel. But we're here to discuss more important things."

Marla joined in, "They have arranged a gathering where all of you can meet again and discuss whatever you want. Don't ask me how or why, but gatherings of this kind are rare, indeed. Yet, for some reason, it was arranged for you. Remember, 'unto everything there is a time and a season'? If we don't go now, it would be another decade or two before the timing would be right again." She looked at Gideon as if to say, it's time to go.

"Wait," I said, "who are 'they' and what is this gathering?" Dream or no dream, I was becoming a bit apprehensive.

"Not to worry," replied Gideon, "you'll see. You've been waiting for this for a long while. You'll meet them soon. Let's go."

"Hold it," I insisted, "at least let me get dressed. I'll put on my... ." Before I could say anything else, I glanced at the mirror across the room, recognizing that I was already fully clothed.

"That's what happens in this state of awareness, John," said Marla as she held one of my arms and Gideon the other. In what could be described as a blink of an eye, we were flying above the ground, soaring without wings. There was a sense of uncommon freedom as I felt the wind on my face. Yes, I did recall doing this a number of times before. This was fun and I made myself a promise to practice it more often. It couldn't have been more than a minute before we landed feet first, Mary Poppins style, in a green meadow surrounded by large trees. The light had changed from the bright lights of my room to a softer, more subtle glow produced by the iridescence of a full moon. I really wasn't too sure of anything at this point.

"I don't think there's a full moon tonight," I said to Gideon. "What's a moon doing up there?"

"Different space-time, John," he replied. "Different level of awareness. Some of the old rules you know don't apply here. This is one of those in-between places where worlds intersect." Before he could continue, we heard voices coming from the clearing.

Suddenly I heard a voice say, "Hello, John. Glad you could make it." I continued searching ahead into the clearing as Gideon, Marla and I walked toward the voice. The light gradually increased in intensity until I could see clearly. Then there was the sound of thunder as the entire area lit up as bright as day. I covered my eyes for a moment and when I opened them, I saw two people walking toward me. As I stared at the smiling faces and recognized who they were, my legs went limp and Gideon and Marla literally had to hold me up. I heard myself mumbling incoherently over and over again as they approached.

Chapter Thirteen

Once upon a Dream

There are times in life when you aren't sure of anything, times when you feel betrayed by your own senses. This certainly seemed to be one. At first, I thought this was an ordinary dream with part of me sleeping peacefully while another part of me was involved in dream adventures. I've had such dreams before where I knew I was dreaming and understood that in the morning I'd remember everything and would smile and reflect upon these mysteries. But what I was now experiencing seemed so real that I instinctively knew this was much more than a dream.

I continued staring at the people approaching me. It was Pandayji who had called my name and there, next to him, was Mardai. She seemed as young and beautiful as the day we were married many, many years ago. She put her arm around me and said, "I bet you're surprised. I'm so happy that we can be together again, even though it's only for a short while."

"It's so good to see you. I've missed you terribly over the years," I said, "I do see you from time to time in my dreams, but I don't ever remember seeing you as clearly as now. In fact, this doesn't even seem like a dream." I thought how quickly one accepts and adapts to events in dreams.

"It's not a dream, my dear John," she smiled sweetly, "it's as real as you are. But it won't last very long and it won't happen again like this for quite a number of years. Let's go see the kids." As she said this, the brightness of the scene dimmed to that of a lovely, pale moonlight, bright enough to see by, but not so bright as to be uncomfortable.

"Kids? What kids?" I asked in surprise.

"Our kids, silly." She giggled as she took my hand, just like she used to, and led me to a spot behind a clump of trees. Pandayji remained behind with Marla and Gideon, engrossed in conversation.

"What are our kids doing here? And how come Pandayji is here?" I questioned.

Before she could answer, I saw Malika and Jonathan in the moonlight. "Hi Dad," shouted

Malika, "we wanted to surprise you, but Jonathan gave it away."

"No Dad," Jonathan countered, "she spoiled the surprise. Mom told us you'd be here."

I greeted them as if this sort of thing occurred everyday. Rather puzzled, I asked, "Your mom told you I'd be here?"

"Oh yes," said Malika, "we visit with Mommy often. She tells us lots of things whenever we see her." I knew I shouldn't have asked.

They walked over to chat with Pandayji. I looked at them, then at Mardai and thought that this is the first time in years I've seen the entire family together. While part of me knew this meeting was temporary, I wanted to soak up and relish every moment.

"They seem so happy." said Mardai. "In a way, I never really left them. I visit whenever I can and I still try to teach them as much as possible. They're used to meeting me like this. I never left you, either. Malika and Jonathan will probably remember this event in different versions of a dream. Pandayji will also have vague recollections of a dream. Right now he is discussing some important matters with Marla and Gideon."

"They know each other?" I asked.

"Of course, they do," she replied, "many of us belong to the same large family and we get together from time to time to catch up with what's been going on. Pandayji has always been like a brother to us. Don't you remember how he helped during the complex adoption procedures for Malika and Jonathan? Without him, I doubt whether we could have accomplished such a giant task. When the judge issued the final adoption decrees, Marla and Gideon were standing right behind him. Then there's the one known as Butch. A unique bond exists between the two of you that creates magic in other's lives. All of us have known each other forever, it seems. And there are others whom you may not recognize at first, but who are, nevertheless, a part of our reality."

Mardai sat down on the grass and motioned me to sit next to her. "It's as if you've never been gone," I said. "Seems like only yesterday that you and I and the children were doing just what we're doing here. I've often wondered where you were and what you were doing. Everyday I prayed that you'd be happy and peaceful in your new surroundings and that, wherever you were, your life would be an inspiration to others as it was here."

"Never stop praying for those who have gone on. The prayers are heard and answered. We feel the warm glow of love whenever someone prays," she replied.

"Have you met with the others? I mean our parents and other friends and family who have died?" I asked.

"No one dies," she replied, "they just change realities. Different rules apply when they go through the door called 'death.' When your star sets on one horizon, it simultaneously rises on another. Each higher reality has laws, which transcend and include the laws of the previous one. So, here we have laws that you aren't aware of yet. For example, time and space have different meanings for us. They are not a restriction like they were in Earth reality. Yes, I am with the others often. We work together on some joint projects, like helping new arrivals to adjust. We're as close as ever, in fact, much closer than we used to be. We all have common, non-conflicting goals and are bound together by golden strands of love and caring." She was silent for a moment as if lost in reflection.

"Your mom and dad visit you often in your dreams. Mine are there, too. We all help and guide you in your Earth life as much as we're permitted, you know. However, there's a non-interference clause which sometimes restricts our ability to help; it's more a matter of degrees of helping rather than total exclusion. And we're there with the children, too. We all have joint projects that span dimensions and realities."

"So many times I thought you'd forgotten us," I said. "I felt, that because your work was finished here, you just went on to other things that were more interesting and, perhaps, even more productive. Not that I expected you to be here with us and dedicate yourself to our well-being, but every once in a while, every once in a long while, I thought I'd hear a comforting word or some cheers of encouragement. I guess I felt so alone, yet, I kept on keeping on. What could I do? They finally foreclosed on the house and nearly repossessed the car. Many times they turned off the water and telephone services and, well, you just wouldn't believe it. I was even involved in a serious car accident and totally wrecked the car."

"Interesting that you hadn't noticed how you walked away from that car wreck with just minor bruises," she replied with a touch of sadness in her voice. "You're still living in a house. The car was not repossessed. Water and telephone services were restored within hours, no health challenges, no major catastrophes. And look at Jonathan and Malika. Malika graduated from high school with honors and has completed college on a full scholarship. She has grown up to be a wonderful, beautiful young woman. Jonathan has become quite a young man, also. He is going to college and is trying to make up his mind about his future. And he is loved and respected by many. Both have grown to be loving, caring, responsible... look at them... ," as she pointed in their direction.

"Look at them, John," she continued, "you couldn't ask for better. I know it's been rough, but you've been doing a wonderful job. We've helped as best we could. And we'll be there for you and the children. I never stopped loving and caring for all of you. I always respond to your call when you hold me in your thoughts. We are all there for you, but we, too, have other things to do. You just don't feel our presence as strongly as you should. But it doesn't matter. Just keep on doing what you're doing and you'd be amazed how things have a way of working out. You'll see that although morning takes all night coming, surely it does come."

I sat overcome in a mixture of joy and sadness, trying to make this moment last forever. She must have sensed my thoughts for she leaned over and placed her head on my shoulder and said, "Don't try to make things stay as they are. Life is a process that changes constantly. You've heard the old saying, 'Life is not the candle nor the flame. It's the burning.' Of necessity, this moment will pass, but there will be new moments, perhaps, more glorious ones."

"Do we meet like this often?" I asked, not knowing quite what to say.

"Not exactly like this. But we do meet. You'll remember this meeting for a long time. The other meetings are just like dreams to you, but no less valid. Those you may not remember and, if you do, they are very faint and somewhat vague. This meeting was arranged so you could see and experience how reality is different in different states of consciousness. And naturally, I wanted you to know that I've never abandoned you, I've never left you. I am always around when you need me."

My emotions crested as I blurted out, "Why did you leave me and the children so soon? When you died, our entire world came to a grinding halt. They were so young. You were so young. You suffered so much. I was hoping that we'd grow old together. Then you left and it's never been the same since."

"I was wondering when you'd get around to that. It wasn't that anyone was picking on you and the kids, John," she answered. "It was all a part of the grand plan that we agreed upon long before we were born. My work on Earth was finished. I had to leave so that you could fulfill your mission. My suffering taught you compassion in a way that you'd never forget. Whether you realize it or not, I'm still a help to you now. I can do lots more from where I am. There's a wonderful pattern in all of this. But sometimes patterns don't make much sense while they're being woven. Our emotions can cloud our perception and understanding. Eventually, you'll see the beauty of the whole thing. Don't analyze everything so much. Some experiences like joy, peace, love, faith and hope do not lend themselves easily to analysis. It's enough to know that we *do not, cannot* die. We are bound by ties that stretch from eternity to the shores of forever."

"Yeah, I guess so," I replied as I reflected on what she was saying. "Sometimes it does seem unfair, though," I murmured more to myself than to her.

"In what way, John?" she innocently asked.

"Well, take this financial thing, for example. You'd think that by this time in life I'd have had it all put together. I certainly work hard, but often I see the good suffer and the evil prosper. And I cry out to the heavens like the Psalmist of old, 'How long, O Lord? How long?' But silence, eternal silence. Sometimes I think that we should pray, 'Our Father Who art in heaven, stay there for all the good it does!' Yep! Doesn't make sense sometimes."

"Oh, you poor thing!" she said in mock horror, "to think that life is unfair! Listen, John, life isn't fair or unfair. Life just *is*. What you call your financial problems are at an end now. You'll see the reasons for that challenge later on."

"What do you mean 'at an end'? They're not at an end. Look at what's been happening."

"They're almost over. You'll see. Gideon will explain it to you soon."

"Sure, he'll explain. Just like he was going to explain the greatest secret in the Universe," I cracked somewhat sarcastically.

"If answers are provided for every question, their impact is temporary and easily dismissed. But if answers are discovered in the experience of life, their influence continues for a long time. We believe much more of what we have personally experienced than what others could ever tell us. Gideon and Marla love you very much and seek only your highest good. They will continue to help you."

At the mention of Marla's name, my mind raced back to our romantic interlude. A twinge of guilt came over me as I sat wondering what Mardai might have thought about it. She must have known what was on my mind for she said, "There are areas of your life that are exclusively and personally your own. Even I do not get involved there. Just live your life as brilliantly as possible and don't let guilt, regret or fear negate your validity as a child of the Infinite. There's no need to feel guilty about you and Marla or you and anyone else."

With a sigh of relief, I asked, "I really would like to know more about this after-life world, Mardai. Would you help me learn more?"

"First of all, John, there isn't a before or even an after-life as you think of it. There is only one life with various aspects. A continuation of life, if you will. Certainly I could tell you more, but you don't need to know that right now. Live the life you're familiar with the best way possible and all other aspects—before and after—will fall into place."

Suddenly, the children ran up to us, happy and laughing. "We've got to go back now," said Malika, "so, bye Mom, bye Dad. See you again soon." They hugged us, turned around and slowly faded into nothingness.

"They had to return to their bodies, John," Mardai commented. "We must go, too. Come, let's join the others."

She noticed my sadness as we walked back to the spot where Gideon, Marla and Pandayji were still talking. "Listen, my dear John," she said, "in this great now and then and this fantastic here and there, we'll meet each other wherever and whenever you want to go over things that bother you, or just to visit to be with each other. It won't be exactly like we met here, but will, nevertheless, be as wonderful. On this visit, you'll remember every detail. Most other visits will be more dream-like in nature."

"Why?" I objected, "I want to remember everything."

"That's not always wise, John," she replied. "If it happened too often, it's possible to confuse realities. It would be like trying to listen to two radio stations at once or watching two television shows at the same time. You couldn't focus properly on either. Don't worry. I'll be close when you think of me."

"Will you say 'Hello' to my mom and dad and yours also? Tell them I love them."

"They know you love them, John. We feel love very strongly here. They love you, too, and meet with you, from time to time to exchange thoughts and impart gems of wisdom. When you need to talk to them, hold them strongly in your thoughts and speak as if they were standing near you. Instantly you'll be in touch. Know that you are well loved."

By the time we had reached the others, I suddenly felt an overwhelming tiredness come over me. I yawned and said, "Excuse me."

Everyone was now looking at me and smiling. The last thing I remembered was Mardai saying to me, "Don't worry anymore about the financial situation. It's being taken care of... that challenge is about over. Sleep well and... ."

Chapter Fourteen

The Ambrose Stone

The sound of the phone awakened me from what must have been a very deep sleep. I reached over and grabbed the handset only to find that it was my wake-up call, heralding me to face a new day. The last thing I remembered before falling asleep last night was being in a green meadow with Mardai, the children, Pandayji, Gideon and Marla. How real it seemed then, but now, with daylight streaming through the windows, my rational mind rebelled. It continuously repeated that a dream is a dream is a dream and stories told in the night had no relevance to my waking hours.

As I sat on the edge of the bed pondering, a part of me knew better and reflected on the events of last night. In an instant I remembered everything—the meadow, the moonlight, the visit with Mardai—all vividly rushed back with such force that I could hardly sit still. I must see Pandayji and hear his version of what happened. Gideon and Marla also had some explaining to do.

His flexible schedule allowed Pandayji to be able to spend a great deal of time with me in Bombay and even to travel with me to other parts of India, if necessary. I've always been amazed at his wide range of friends. From princes to peasants, from intellectuals to illiterates, Pandayji was loved and respected by many people. Not even the Holy Ones of the Himalayas nor the high and the mighty of Hyderabad could refuse him. He was both a loyal and influential friend and I was, indeed, fortunate to have him share his time with me.

In about half an hour we were scheduled to meet at the Samarkand Café, a part of the hotel complex. I glanced at the clock on the nightstand and knew I had to rush. Refreshed by a quick shower, it wasn't long before I found myself striding through the lobby, approaching the doors of the Samarkand. At this early hour it was relatively uncrowded. I spotted him at a table in the far corner. He saw me coming, smiled and said, "Good morning, John, I trust that you slept well last night. Those long flights could be so tiring, especially crossing so many time zones."

"Good to see you again, Pandayji," I replied as I seated myself across from him. I was anxious to ask him about his experiences in the meadow, but thought I'd wait a while. Over breakfast, we discussed my schedule for the week and agreed there would be enough free time to visit some interesting sites in the north, if I felt like it. Still not a word from him about last night, so I brought up the subject. Since I wasn't sure whether the whole event was the result of my overactive imagination, I was rather cautious in my approach. "I had some weird things happen last night, Pandayji," I said.

He looked up immediately and said, "Your room wasn't comfortable? I'll speak with them."

"No, not my room, Pandayji. Just some dreams I think," I replied.

He creased his forehead, as if trying to recall, and said, "Now that I think of it, I, too, had some dreams in which you and Mardai, Jonathan and Malika were present. But I can't remember anything else. Seems like others were there, too."

"What others?" I asked, "Gideon and Marla?"

"I know them through your books, John, and yet, I've never personally met them. There's a familiarity with the names, but really, I have no idea who else might have been in my dream. And even if I had met Gideon and Marla, I wouldn't have known who they were." He smiled and said that he had slept well and was sorry he couldn't remember the rest of his dream. However, I knew he believed dreams were important and had a beneficial effect on our daily lives. Mardai was right, I thought. Pandayji forgot that he had met us last night. Then he asked me what my dream was about.

"Well," I replied, "I saw Mardai and the children. Gideon and Marla were there too, but the strangest thing was that you were there speaking with Gideon and Marla. To me, it was more than a dream, Pandayji. It was so real... as real as our sitting here right now. Perhaps, it wasn't a dream at all. Perhaps, it really happened."

"There are many mysteries on Earth, John," he said, "many dimensions to life. We probably exist in all these dimensions simultaneously. But I think we only remember them vaguely so that we don't confuse them."

Breakfast was finished and it was time to go about the business I had traveled so far to accomplish. Pandayji had taken care of all the arrangements, so my appointments went smoothly—so smoothly in fact, that we had much of the day remaining for whatever we wanted. "Why don't you get some rest? You must still be somewhat tired. We can meet later for dinner," he said as his car pulled up to my hotel. That sounded fine to me, so I nodded in agreement.

"Would about seven o'clock be fine? At the Samarkand?" he asked as I stepped out.

"That would be great," I replied, waving good-bye.

"See you then," he said and as an after-thought added, "It would really be nice to meet this Gideon and Marla one day."

I smiled, "One day, perhaps," and walked into the hotel. A little rest would do me good. In a few minutes I was in my suite and about to close my eyes, when a knock sounded at the door. I should have placed the "Do Not Disturb" sign on the doorknob, I thought while getting up to see who was there. I never open a hotel door without checking to see who's on the other side.

"Who is it?" I asked.

"Gideon and Marla," came the reply.

I threw open the door to welcome my two friends. "We won't stay long," said Gideon, "just wanted to remind you that we'll be here for a few days, in case you didn't hear me say it last night. With all the excitement of seeing Mardai again, you may have been confused and thought it was all just a dream."

"Come on in," I insisted, "at least stay for a little while."

They entered and Gideon took the easy chair while Marla sat in a lotus-pose on the floor. "So, it wasn't a dream after all," I mused.

"No, John," said Marla, "it wasn't a dream. You always ask about her so, it was time that Mardai, herself, told you how she was."

"It was great to see her again, but it was totally unexpected. She explained a number of things and said that you would tell me about my financial situation and how best to handle it. And, of course, there's this great secret you keep mentioning. I'm so tired of hearing about it. Isn't it about time that you tell me what it is?" I looked from Marla to Gideon and back again.

"We'll see you at dinner to discuss some of this," Gideon said.

"Pandayji will be meeting me for dinner. I'm sure he'd love to meet both of you. You were having a long conversation with him last night and, yet, he didn't seem to remember either of you this morning."

"Thus far," replied Gideon, "he has only seen us in his dreams. At dinner this evening, he will get to see us with you. Not to worry. It'll be fun."

Both of them stood up as Gideon continued, "We'll see ourselves out. Don't bother getting up."

Marla leaned over and gave me a gentle peck on my lips. She smiled at me, winked and said, "Remember what she said to you last night."

They turned, walking clear through the locked door. "Must be great to do that," I thought as I fell asleep right there on the sofa.

When I awoke it was almost time for dinner, so I hastily prepared and headed off to the Samarkand. It would be wonderful, I thought, for all of us to be together. My friends and acquaintances have rarely, or ever, seen Gideon or Marla and I couldn't help wondering why an exception was made for Pandayji.

In a few minutes, I was walking toward the restaurant when I heard Pandayji's voice call out, "Hello, John. Over here."

I looked toward the voice and saw Pandayji and an old, bearded man standing next to one of the large columns that stood throughout the lobby. "Hi, Pandayji," I said as I walked over to them.

"John," said Pandayji, "I want you to meet an old friend of mine. He's known as the Boatman of Pondicherry and is in town for just a few days."

"Hi, Mr... er... Hi... ," I said as I stretched out my hand toward the Boatman, "it's good to meet you," I continued, "what did you say your name was?"

"Just call me Boatman," he said with a mischievous grin. "Over the years, Panday, here, has told me so much about you. In a way, I feel as though I know you."

Being a poor judge of age, I guessed the Boatman to be somewhere in his mid to late seventies. His beard, long and white, flowed halfway down his chest, complimenting his shoulder-length, gray hair. He was dressed in a long saffron colored robe with a blue headband circling his forehead. He seemed to be in excellent physical condition. Although he was definitely of Indian lineage, his deep, resonant voice spoke impeccable English with a slight British accent.

"It's so good to see you, John," he continued, looking straight into my eyes.

"What a beautiful accent you have," I said, following quickly with, "Will you please join us for dinner?"

"Not tonight, thank you," he replied. "And the accent is left-over from my Oxford and Cambridge days."

I turned to Pandayji and pleaded, "Pandayji, please make him stay. Gideon and Marla will also be joining us for dinner. It would be wonderful for all of us. Please, it won't be any problem."

Pandayji's eyes lit up as he heard that Gideon and Marla would join us. "Why don't you stay for dinner, Boatman? It would be nice to meet John's other friends."

"I really would like to," replied Boatman, "But I have some appointments to keep. If more people would walk on water, there would be no need for boatmen, or," and he laughed, "if you prefer, boat persons. However, I have a little gift for you, John"

He handed me a small package wrapped in lovely blue paper. "Take this," he said, "I think you've been looking for it for a long time. It's only a tiny gift, but I wanted you to have it. But you must promise me you won't open it until dinner."

"Thank you," I said as I took the gift, "Thank you. I promise I won't open it till then. I wish you could stay."

"I must go now," he replied. "I'll probably see you again before you leave. But if not, then sometime, somewhere." He turned to Pandayji saying, "Thank you, Panday, for giving me the opportunity to meet him. I'm very grateful. See you soon." He bowed, turned and left.

As he disappeared from view, I said somewhat wistfully, "I wish I could have gotten to know him better; seems like such an intriguing chap. And to think, he even brought me a gift. So kind of him, Pandayji. I wonder what's in the box."

"Remember," said Pandayji, "you promised to wait."

"Until dinner then," I replied.

"I am so excited about meeting Gideon and Marla, John," said Pandayji, "I didn't know they were here."

"They travel a lot," I replied. "You never know when you'll bump into them. I only knew that they were here when they stopped by my hotel. I'm sure you'll enjoy their company."

"I bet I will," said Pandayji.

"Let's wait for them in the restaurant."

We walked to the Samarkand and were ushered to a table for four near a window overlooking the sea.

"Remember this table, John? This is where you, Mardai and I sat many times, years ago."

"Yes," I replied, "seems familiar but feels like it was a century ago."

"Now you may open your gift from Boatman. It's dinner time."

"You're right. Let's see what it is before Gideon and Marla arrive." With that, I tore off the wrapper. In my hand was a small, beautifully crafted, wooden box that carried the faint odor of cedar. I gently opened it to find a small velvet pouch in the center. I held the pouch, which felt like it contained a solid object. Pandayji leaned closer as I inverted the pouch and gingerly extracted its contents. There, in the palm of my hand, was a smooth stone about the size of a walnut, somewhat oblong in shape with a faint, grayish, green color. I looked at it more closely and saw there were letters carved into it.

"Look, Pandayji," I exclaimed, "it's a stone with the word... oh, this can't be... Pandayji, this is impossible... no, no it just can't be. Would you believe this Pandayji? Look what's written here. It says... this is something else..."

"What, John? For heaven's sake, what does it say?"

"See for yourself," I stammered, "it says AMBROSE. It's the Ambrose Stone. Pandayji, this can't be, can it?"

I handed the stone to Pandayji who examined it with wary eyes. "I've heard about this stone and its magical qualities. But why did Boatman bring it to you?"

"I haven't the foggiest idea, Pandayji. Years ago, my dad told me about this stone. I spent considerable time and energy trying to locate it. I remember my dad said something of hearing about the stone from an old man who lived by the river."

"Well, Boatman lives by a river. Could it be that he's the old man your dad told you about?"

"Couldn't be," I said, "my dad never visited this country. How could he have met Boatman?"

"Hello there, anybody home?" rang a familiar voice. Both Pandayji and I were so focused on the stone that we hadn't noticed Gideon and Marla standing next to our table.

"Pandayji," I said as I held the stone, replacing it in its pouch, "I want you to meet my dear friends, Gideon and Marla."

Chapter Fifteen

If You Plant a Redwood Tree...

Pandayji rarely gets flustered as his work brings him in touch with all sorts of people. He is as comfortable speaking with peasants in the planting fields as delivering a moving speech to crowds of thousands. Through the auspices of Pandayji, I have met government leaders and top celebrities in his country and, yet, in the presence of Gideon and Marla, he appeared as a little schoolboy seeing his hero, face to face for the first time.

"Hi Pandayji," said Gideon as he reached over and shook Pandayji's outstretched hand, "it's great to see you again."

"Again? Whatever do you mean, sir?" Pandayji looked puzzled, "unfortunately, I don't recall ever meeting you before."

Marla walked over to Pandayji, shook his hand and said, "You may not remember meeting us, but I assure you, we know you well. John speaks of you often. And, of course, we see you from time to time when we visit the Holy Ones. Sometimes we meet during dream time."

"You certainly understand these things, Pandayji," Gideon added. "Anyone who spends so much time with the Holy Ones will understand who we are and what we're about."

By this time we were all sitting comfortably around the table. Having possession of the Ambrose Stone after all these years caused me to squirm with excitement. I was anxious to share its story with Gideon. From the corner of my eye, I could see Pandayji sitting sponge-like, quietly absorbing everything that was going on. It was as if he was trying to remember long forgotten adventures while reacquainting himself with old companions. I casually glanced at Marla and, again, there was that special alluring sensation at having her so close. We placed our dinner order and casually chatted while it was being served. But the Ambrose Stone, I must get back to it.

"Gideon, do you know what this is?" I asked, hardly able to contain my enthusiasm between bites of the delicate Indian roti. "I mean, this is the most amazing thing that could ever happen. Here, look at it." I handed the pouch containing the Ambrose

Stone to Gideon and waited with anticipation for his response as I reached for my glass of water. Some Indian curries could be very spicy.

As casually as you please, Gideon took the pouch and without even opening it said, "Oh, the Ambrose Stone. Don't tell me the Boatman of Pondicherry was here." His voice was so matter-of-fact, as if this sort of thing happened everyday. I glanced at Marla hoping she would say something to sustain my enthusiasm, but she seemed even less amused by my news.

"That's right, Gideon," she said, "don't you remember Boatman saying something about giving the Ambrose Stone to John? But that was quite a while back."

"Ah, now I remember," replied Gideon turning to me, "of course, John, the Ambrose Stone. You've wanted to have it since you were a little boy. How could I have forgotten? You thought it would perform miracles for you. You know, John," he said wistfully, "I think you might still believe the Ambrose Stone is a magic genie."

"Well, isn't it? Isn't that why this stone is legendary?" I asked somewhat disappointed by their lack of appreciation.

"Oh John," Marla replied, "don't you know by now that the magic is not in the stone? It's not in the sky, the water or the trees. The magic is in *you*. It's been there all along. This stone or crystals, icons, crosses, beads, rabbits' foot and all other symbols are just that—symbols of something else, something far superior. The magic of the Ambrose Stone is only a reflection, and a poor one at that, of the true magic of your being."

My spirit fell. After all these years, I now had possession of the magical stone only to discover that there was no magic in the stone after all. Was my father deceived by the stories he had heard? Was the old man who lived by the river just a tale repeated by parents to enchant little children? And yet, it seemed that Gideon knew the Boatman, or else knew of him. Were there no mysteries left in the universe, no magic after all? My facial expression changed, sinking to an image of de-jection. Pandayji patted me on the shoulder and said, "I, too, have heard stories of this stone. Perhaps, they were only legends, but I have heard that myths and legends have their origins in some form of truth. Who knows, John, maybe the legends were just over-exaggerated."

"It is the *belief* in the power of the Stone that creates the magic," said Gideon. "The power of belief is one of the most powerful potions available. The stone or any other talisman is just a focal point for your beliefs. Believe that you inhabit a magical world and the world is full of magic. On the other hand, believe that you live in an evil empire and everything will work together to prove you right." He ceremoniously passed the pouch back to me.

"It's a wonderful momento, John," said Marla. "Perhaps you should keep it in a conspicuous place on your desk to remind you of its meaning. Discover the power that is already within you and you'll never need the Ambrose Stone to validate who you are."

I was sad. Here I was surrounded by wonderful friends, but feeling dejected because of a stone—a piece of rock. Gideon's voice broke into my thoughts. He must have noticed my long face. "Your disappointment is due to your feeling that there is no magic in the rock, John. But it doesn't mean that the rock was useless. It served and still serves as a concentrator of immense energy. For example, long ago in England, I saw King Richard Coeur de Lion use it to regain his crown. With the belief in the power of the Ambrose, the hordes of Genghis Khan were able to march across the face of most of the civilized world. The ancient Egyptians built great pyramids with its help. Gandhi used it to bring freedom to his country. All of them knew that the power was within themselves, but it expressed itself through the instrument of the Ambrose Stone."

"Perhaps, this is like that greatest secret you're always going to tell me about. Lots of noise and no substance." I was on a roll and didn't hold back. "Here," I continued, "we have Pandayji with us. He's been so excited at the prospect of meeting the two of you that he could hardly wait. Yet, we sit here talking about some silly stone." I continued as they sat, patiently enduring my self-pitying monologue. I spoke of the long, hard journey toward success, about ridiculous dreams of birds reading books, how we put our trust in the wrong things and how, even after doing everything in our power and doing them right at that, the result still may not turn out as we expected. I gloried in self-pity—how financial problems had made it so difficult to achieve success or to enjoy anything, how it has been so long and, yet, no major changes.

While concluding my ranting and raving session, I became embarrassed that Pandayji had been held witness to such an unenlightened outburst. "Well, there!" I said. "I feel better now, much better. It was marvelous marinating in self-pity. Now, watch this!" I picked up the pouch, took out the Ambrose Stone, walked to the open window and, in one final gesture of frustration and disgust, flung it far into the Arabian Sea. Then with tremendous composure I sat down again, looked at my three friends and smiled smugly. "Now what were you saying about finances, Gideon?"

"What finances? Did I say something about finances?" quipped Gideon. Then quickly with a broad grin he offered, "I know, I know. I'll explain. I don't want you throwing me into the water, too."

"To the point and step by step this time, please." I demanded in a commanding tone. "Mardai told me that you'd explain finances... money... . Why has it been a problem for so long? I'm tired, very tired and more than a bit frustrated. I keep wondering how I'm going to take care of my family and pay all those bills. I'll sit here for hours, if necessary, to hear what you have to say. So, say it. Go on, Gideon. Please, start right now. I'm listening."

He was quiet for a few moments, composing himself as he finished the last bit of his dinner.

Then he looked me straight in the eye while proclaiming, "Once you had quite some financial security; then you lost it all and had to start again from ground zero. You were able to start building back again, but have encountered some major ups and downs over the past few years. You..."

Still very annoyed, I interrupted. "Don't recount my financial history, Gideon. I'm all too familiar with it. Just tell me what the problem is, where the solution is and why it's taken so damn long to rectify. Is that too much to ask?"

He didn't let my vexation bother him, but took them in stride and continued unruffled, like a professor explaining a concept to a rather dull student. "For you to know where you are, you have to look at where you've been. And for you to know where you're going, you've got to know where you are. You are at a point now where you'll be reaping the benefits of all the hard work and persistence you've invested in your life. Many times, people think they have a money problem. Instead, they have a problem in coming to themselves and knowing who they are. If your problem seems to be only money, then you do not have a problem."

"There you go again," I interrupted, impatiently. I wanted to know why it's taking so long to pull out of the money mess that has plagued me for too long. But here he was offering me platitudes about reaping benefits, being persistent, always taking another step and a heap of other double talk. "Why don't you get to the point?" I asked. By this time I didn't care whether he struck me with thunderbolts or fried me with lightning.

This time he did not smile. His eyes, normally dancing with laughter and compassion, narrowed to twin slits of ice. I knew that I had sparked a thunderstorm. I've never seen either Gideon or Marla caught up in the throes of anger. I've often wondered whether they're affected by emotions at all, only to discover later that everyone is. It wasn't that Gideon was losing his patience, it was more like his eyes were saying, "Shut up, stop whining and listen to what I have to say." A moment later, those piercing eyes softened to their original state. How well he managed to rein his emotions, I thought. This time I decided to listen without interrupting.

"What I have to say about finances, especially yours, John, will take a little while. Mardai knew what she was saying when she told you those troubles are at an end. You've labored for many years through some very rough times to make it all come together. There were many times when you wanted to give up, but you rested a while and continued. Through it all, you exhibited remarkable courage and persistence. You exhibited tremendous faith and you never let hope die. And yet, nothing seemed to change."

"You're darn right," I interjected, forgetting my resolve to shut up and listen. "Nothing changed. Or, to be more correct, the more things changed, the more they stayed the same."

He pretended not to hear and continued. "Whenever you became very tired or desperate or frustrated, you set up so many energy blocks around you that you couldn't hear nor see the guidance that was always available. You knew in your head that your problem was not raising money but raising consciousness. You knew in your head, but you didn't know it in your heart. You have seen the connection enough times to remember the old saying, 'It's not by might nor by power, but by my Spirit says the Lord.' What you needed wasn't money, you just needed ideas. One good idea could bring you all the money you would ever need. When you're worried or troubled, your anxiety blocks the flow of creative ideas. You then survive at the circumference of life, instead of living at the center of your being."

He paused for a moment and I took the opportunity to ask, "Is this what's been happening all this time?"

Marla replied while Gideon took a sip of his coffee. "In a way, John. In a manner of speaking that's what you were doing, but it isn't the entire story. Bean seeds grow very quickly, produce their crop, then wither away in one season. Redwood trees take much longer to grow, but they last for centuries. Both come from little seeds and both have their place in the larger scheme of things. Because of your nature and because of agreements you've made with yourself at some of the highest levels of your being, you decided not to grow bean plants. Instead, you planted redwood seeds. If you plant redwood seeds, you get redwood trees. It seems like it took forever, but they've finally grown into magnificent, giant trees and the time for resting in their lovely shade is here."

Pandayji had been so engrossed that I was startled to hear him speak. "I think I've had the same problem. Situations are much better now than in recent years. I was getting to the point of accepting mediocrity and settling for a life of financial hardship. Then I met one of the Holy Ones who explained it much as you did, Marla. From that time on, I understood that it wasn't that anything was wrong with me or my choice of career. It was more that ideas, which were blocked were seeking to express themselves through me. Now I let ideas flow freely and I listen in the quietness of my heart for the 'still, small voice' that always whispers which way to go."

"It is the way to go, Pandayji. The Holy Ones know the secrets of the universe," said Gideon. Then he turned to me and continued, "And we'll talk about the greatest secret as soon as the time's right. But that wasn't the whole story about lack and scarcity, John. Many people don't believe they deserve prosperity. They're full of guilt and fear and down in their hearts, the guilt says, 'You don't deserve, you don't deserve. You messed up before. You're not worthy' and the fear says, 'Seek after security. Worship at its temple and you'll be taken care of for the rest of your life.' What they fail to realize is that *there is no security in material things. Security is a state of mind.* Like the man once said, 'Many times I've been broke, but never have I been poor.' Being broke is, generally, a temporary affair. Being poor is a state of mind, a condition of being, if you will. It all leads back to a concept of self."

A waiter cleared the table while another, pushing a food trolley piled with an assortment of decadent pastries, inquired about dessert. Pandayji offered some suggestions to which we all agreed. As we enjoyed dessert, Gideon continued his explanation. "Prosperity is an aspect of the spirit. It is having a consciousness from which all good things flow. There are certain laws that trigger aspects of prosperity. For example, the habit of giving thanks a number of times throughout the day for all the blessings in your life removes much of the debris that prevent free flow along the river of life. Did you know that one of the meanings of the word 'affluence' is free flow?"

"Interesting," I murmured, much calmer now, "I never thought of it that way."

"Here's another law of prosperity. *Whatever your talent or gift is, give it to the world as freely and as joyfully as possible.* The more you give the more you get. You'll find this law well hidden or disguised in the holy books of many religions. You've heard it said, 'Give and it shall be given unto you.' You cannot outgive the Universe. Give of that which you have. Whatever your lot in life, there are many who wish they were in your shoes. Share whatever little you have and it will return to you manifold, in surprising ways."

"Some people feel that they have very little and so, they cannot afford to be generous," I said. "They say it's difficult for them to give when they themselves are struggling to survive. What do you tell them?"

"John, if you find it difficult to share when you have very little, believe me, you will find it ten times more difficult to share when you have plenty. Instead of saying, 'When I am rich, I'll give to others,' give to others first and you'll end up being rich. It doesn't need to be material things. You can share your time, talents, attention or compassion just as you can share your bread. A wise person once wrote a little ditty that goes like this:

A man there was and they called him mad,
The more he gave, the more he had.

"And never give up hope. The word prosperity itself comes from the root word 'prospere,' meaning to go forward in hope. Faith, hope and love will help solve any problem. You don't need faith to have hope, but you need hope to have faith. Hope is the enemy of fear. Fear says you'll fail. Hope says it's possible that you'll succeed. Fear says you'll lose your job. Hope says you'll find a better one. Fear says time is running out. Hope says hang in there a little while longer."

"But why did it take such a long time for me to work out the financial problems, Gideon? Why is it that only now they seem to be coming to an end? I understand all that you've said, or maybe, most of it. I don't think I have much guilt about anything. Sometimes, there's a bit of fear, but as you said, hope drives it away. I love my work and I love to share my gifts. I give as much and as often as I can. And often during the day, I stop what I'm doing and take a minute to be thankful for all the blessings in my life. Where did I go wrong? Am I so blind? I feel I've been doing all the right things."

He smiled and softly said, "Sometimes you may do everything right and things still do not turn out the way you thought they should. That's called life.

It only means that you don't have all the data. If you could only see what's happening in the invisible world, you'd understand that all is well and that all things are working together for good. When you plant a seed, it takes a little time to grow. Remember? Bean seeds grow quickly. Redwoods take much longer. Don't judge yourself too harshly. You've done quite well, actually. Don't give up now."

A loud crash followed by the sound of shattering glass interrupted the peaceful conversation. I quickly glanced at Gideon, turning my head to see what was happening. The sight that greeted me froze my blood for a split second. Rushing toward our table were three of the most fearsome men I've ever seen. I was about to run for cover when Gideon motioned me to remain seated. Marla shot a startled look at Gideon and exclaimed, "It's the Terror of Trivandrum!" Pandayji and I sat frozen in fear, glaring in disbelief at approaching disaster .

Chapter Sixteen

The Terror of Trivandrum

Trivandrum is a little city in the south of India. It faces the sea and, though sweltering during the day, is cooled in the evening by the gentle on-shore breezes that circle the tip of the sub-continent. It was years since I had visited that small city with Pandayji, but I vividly recall the spontaneous, gregarious nature of its population. There were fishermen and farmers, soldiers and sailors; merchants hawking their wares, strangely dressed figures riding horses, shouting at the top of their voices. Yes, Trivandrum was a time warp from another place and time. Effortlessly with adaptability and grace, it spanned the centuries from long before the British Raj to this very day .

Walk down any street in Trivandrum and you'll quickly find that you're in a time machine, jockeying among many eons. Lovely little restaurants and shops are haphazardly quilted along narrow alleys. While nearby in a tavern, rowdy rebels direct from the journals of Kipling or Clive sit quaffing the king's grog. Listen carefully and you may hear them whisper the name that strikes fear in the hearts of those who delight in injustice, those who prey on the less fortunate. I remember Pandayji in a hushed voice mentioning the legend of the Terror of Trivandrum.

Centuries ago the story goes, he was born a prince and was raised in the luxury of the ruling classes. A philosopher as well as a warrior, he grew into a wonderful young man who spent much of his time helping the poor people of his land. Then one day, an evil half-brother who coveted the throne assassinated his father. The young prince was captured and held prisoner in the dungeon by the new king. He subsequently escaped with the help of some loyal warriors, crossing the Vindya hills to set up camp in a remote refuge.

As time went by, he began helping others who had been wronged by those wielding power. He took from the rich and gave to the poor. He and his band of rebels championed the cause of the underdog. In many ways, he was the Robin Hood of the territory. Many years passed, but he never returned as a prince to the kingdom of his father, preferring to spend the rest of his life fighting evil and injustice. No one seemed to remember his real name and, in time, he came to be known as the Terror of Trivandrum. Some say that he never died and is hundreds of years old. Others say the gods rewarded him with immortality because of his good deeds. Still others claim it is his great grandson who has continued the tradition of a modern day Zorro. Whatever the case may be, the legend of the Terror of Trivandrum continues in that ancient city and has traveled far beyond its borders.

Just as I looked nervously at Gideon, Pandayji let out a gasp while three men, dressed in the garb of medieval warriors stormed up to our table. Gideon sat stoically motionless. The three reached our table, stopped, came to attention and saluted. The short one with the handlebar mustache was the first to speak.

"My dear Sahib, Gideon," the words poured forth from his lips, "I bring you greetings! We heard that you'd be here so, I hastened to pay my respects. And lovely Marla, you're as radiant as ever."

Gideon broke into riotous laughter, stood up and embraced him. Marla giggled while the other two stood at attention as Gideon said, "My dear friend, it has been such a very long time. What are you doing here? You really scared the living daylights out of everyone here."

"I apologize for my rough manners, sir, but I just wanted to see you again. When last we met, you helped me restore the property of those poor peasants who were being cheated by the overseer of their village. I've missed you greatly."

Gideon returned to his seat, nodded to Pandayji and me and said, "I want you to meet an old friend of mine. This 'gentleman,' and I use the term loosely, is Prince Kamal, better known as the Terror of Trivandrum, the Scourge of the South." He then turned to the Terror and said, "These are my dear friends, Pandayji and John. And of course, you know the incomparable Marla."

"It's so good to meet you, all of you," said the Terror, "and greetings again, my Lady Marla."

"Kamal, you haven't changed a bit. You're as much a renegade as ever. It's good to see you, but I didn't expect to see you here."

By this time, the restaurant manager accompanied by two guards was fast approaching our table. The Terror, anticipating their appearance, quickly drew a long, sinister sword from his belt. His two companions did the same and would have caused quite a commotion had Gideon not shouted just as quickly, "Put that thing away. It's not needed here." The Terror and his friends slowly sheathed their swords, while glaring at the manager who, by now, must have wished to be somewhere else.

Gideon then apologized to the manager. "Please excuse my friends. They didn't mean any harm. Sorry for the inconvenience and commotion. Anyway, they'll be leaving soon." The manager seemed only too anxious to agree to anything that would return tranquillity to his restaurant. He thanked Gideon, bowed, turned and left with the two nervous guards in tow.

Marla spoke up, "You always seem to have this effect on others, Kamal. Maybe, you might try to be a bit more cordial? No need to scare others to death. There's enough fear and anger already. We need more light, not more heat." Then she smiled her sweetest smile at him.

"You know that I could never really hurt an innocent person, Milady. They scare themselves because of who they think I am," he replied.

Finally gathering up enough courage to speak, I offered, "Mr. Terror," and was immediately struck with how stupid that sounded. I continued, nevertheless, "are the legends about you true? Some say you were born hundreds of years ago."

He looked at me for a moment, then turned to Gideon as if asking permission to answer. Gideon gave a slight nod and the Terror smiled and said, "My dear sir, all legends have their birth in truth somewhere, once upon a time. I was born Kamal, Prince of the Eastern Territories. But that was a long time ago. My mission is to right wrongs and help the helpless. Allah be praised! I am but his humble servant. My followers and I ride the back of the dangerous winds and, by the beard of the Prophet, we will not rest until justice has been served."

"We have heard of the Terror," said Pandayji to me. "They speak of him in large towns and little villages across the nation. It's said that if you've lost all hope, call upon him in your heart and he will hear you. He would then dispatch a band of his warriors to help rectify your problem. Some say that Lord Rama on his visit to Lankha was given help along the way by the Terror of Trivandrum."

"This whole story seems so confusing," I replied as Kamal beamed a disarming, boyish grin, "it seems as if you're ageless. They speak as if you were born centuries ago. And yet, you don't appear to be a day older than I. I just don't understand."

"Things are not always what they seem to be, my boy," replied the Terror. "Gideon taught us that appearances could be deceiving. People are afraid of what they do not understand. And when they're afraid, they want to destroy or run away. When you're afraid of your enemies, you'll seek to destroy them or hide from them. But when you understand who you are and that you could never be destroyed, when you start living life with hope, spontaneity and joy, you'll find that life flows through you with peace, plenty and power. Prosperity becomes yours. As was said long ago, 'Your enemies are those of your own household.' Mostly, they are your own fears and thoughts."

"Then why do you go around terrorizing?" I asked. "Don't you think there are better ways of solving problems?"

"It's the game," he replied, "I would surely be destroyed by boredom had it not been for this game. We all play some kind of game. This is my game and I love it. Never a dull moment. Others play money games or relationship games or whatever. I prefer this one. Every game has its own rules. If you find that you don't like the game or its rules, instead of sitting down and whining about how unfair the game is—just change it. Look at it from a different point of view or just rewrite the rules. Sometimes people get trapped in their own games and do not realize that they can stop the game at any point. It's all in the interpretation of a point of view, my boy."

A warrior and a philosopher at the same time, what a combination I thought.

"I will go now," he said as he snapped to attention. "Much to be done. Duty calls and all that. It was wonderful seeing you again, Gideon. And Marla, I still wish to take you away and make you my princess. Are you sure you ...?"

Marla interrupted, "Not this time, Kamal. But keep trying; I like it."

"I bid you good evening, John," he said. Then he looked at Pandayji and continued, "It was good to see you, Pandayji. Let us get together in Trivandrum soon. There is a quaint tavern across from the main market. I'll meet you there."

He bowed to Marla, took her hand, kissed it gently, turned to Gideon, saluted and with a flourish, walked straight out with his companions following close behind. It took a few seconds for all that had just happened to sink in. I looked around and saw the few remaining patrons of the restaurant sitting quietly, enjoying their meals as if nothing had happened. I glanced at Pandayji who sat smiling, as if such occurrences were commonplace. I looked at Gideon and asked, "What's the meaning of all that?"

"Meaning? How you love to analyze. Does everything have to have an obvious meaning?" he countered.

"Well, yes," I replied, "I think so."

"Sometimes meanings are not apparent for a long time," he said. "Of course, it's the tendency of some people to try to read all sorts of interpretations into every event. There are times, my dear John, when it's best to enjoy or endure an event for its own sake. A friend of mine, Sigmund, once had a discussion with Marla and me about just such an occurrence. The conclusion was, sometimes a cigar is just a cigar."

"So all this brouhaha was just for nothing? Just a lot of smoke and no fire?"

"No," he replied emphatically, "it was not a lot of noise, not without substance. He was an old, loyal friend just visiting in his own way. That, in itself, was very touching. Do you have to totally analyze everything you do, John? When you eat an apple, do you weigh it, check its color and the texture of its skin? Do you have it sent to a lab for an analysis of nutrients? Sometimes an apple is just an apple. Enjoy it. Kamal and I go way back. He always had an eye for Marla and she could play the flirt, too, when she felt like it. But he's been doing a wonderful work. Many have been helped and given a new lease on life because the Terror of Trivandrum intervened. Don't judge him by the way he looks or how he speaks. People tend to judge by appearances. Learn, as Jesus said, to judge not by appearances."

"I'm sorry, Gideon," I said rather contritely. "I certainly don't want you to think I'm picking on him. I just wanted some answers."

"The problem isn't with the answers," he said. "Answers, you've got. It's the questions you haven't figured yet." He turned to Marla and continued, "Marla, it's getting late for John and Pandayji. They've had an exciting day. Perhaps they should get some rest soon."

"That's a good idea," said Marla. "Enough is enough for one day."

By this time, the restaurant was quite empty and quiet. You never would have guessed that just a short while before, the Terror of Trivandrum stood right here before us. That, perhaps, is the stuff that legends are made of. We left our seats as Pandayji said to Gideon and Marla, "I am grateful to John for finally making it possible to meet the two of you. Thank you so much for dinner. Perhaps, we shall meet again one day."

"Perhaps," replied Gideon. "And keep close to the Holy Ones. They will always guide you in the true way." He pointed to me as he continued. "John here is still wondering what the greatest secret in the universe is while, all the time, it's right under his nose. Next time I see him, I'll share it with him." Gideon shook his head and then as an after thought, added, "as if he doesn't already know it."

"He always speaks in riddles, Pandayji," I said as Marla and Gideon waved goodnight saying they would see me again soon. I said good-bye to Pandayji, promising to meet him for breakfast. In a short while I was back in my room preparing for bed. It had been an extremely interesting evening, and with thoughts of the Terror of Trivandrum, I fell asleep.

During the next few days I wrapped up my work with the ever-present help of Pandayji. He accompanied me to the airport and it wasn't long before it was time to board my plane. I hadn't seen Gideon and Marla since dinner that evening. But that was their way with me, popping in and out of my life and never staying long enough for me to get completely used to their presence.

It was sad saying good-bye to my dear friend Pandayji. We promised to keep in touch more regularly. The speaker blared that my flight was ready for boarding. "Take good care of yourself, Pandayji," I said, "I'll be seeing you again, soon." In a few moments, I was walking down the ramp into the belly of the big metal bird that would soon be flying me back home. My trip to the former Jewel in the Crown had come to an end.

Chapter Seventeen

The Greatest Secret in the Universe

A few weeks had gone by since my return from the land of mysteries. To me, this ancient place always conjured up visions of fiercely armed warriors charging across the plains to do battle with opposing armies. It is interesting to observe how some of the most awesome experiences of one's life could quickly fade into vague memories. Such was the case with my Indian "adventures" as I fell into the routine of daily life again.

Every now and then I'd think of Gideon and Marla. But they, too, didn't command prime time on my daily priority list. There were more pressing duties, like completing a manuscript and beginning a new one, preparing for a lecture tour, buying new shoes for Jonathan, helping Malika fix a flat tire, refinancing my business and countless other activities all competing for my time and attention.

This day, I was quietly relaxing on my back porch, half-asleep, dimly observing the activities of the wildlife in the back yard. It had been a rather hectic day and I felt a few minutes of relaxation before dinner would do me some good. Exhausted, I must have dozed off for the next thing I remember hearing was someone calling my name. I opened my eyes to the sight of Gideon and Marla standing before me.

"Greetings!" said Gideon, "didn't want to wake you, but we have to talk. Can you spare a few minutes?"

Before I could answer, Marla came over, gave me a big hug and gently kissed me on the cheek. "It's been a few weeks, John, but we needed to get together with you."

Now, I was wide-awake, wondering about the urgency of their visit. "I've missed both of you," I said, as they each took a chair, "and I trust all has been well. But why the big hurry to talk to me?"

"We just came from a meeting with the Chief," said Gideon. "You remember? The Big Chief? The Creator of the Universe? Alpha and Omega? Remember meeting Him years ago?"

"How could I forget? Still seems like a strange dream," I answered. "Once on a sailing ship, then in an office in the Big City and another time at a party gathering. Both of you, too. It all seemed quite real."

"It was as real as you could get," Marla said, "more real than breathing. The Chief wants us to explain to you, as clearly and simply as possible, the greatest secret in the universe."

"So, what's the big rush? You waited long enough," I blurted, as I sprang from my chair, waving my hand in the air. "I was beginning to think you'd just made up the whole thing and frankly, I was a bit tired of asking and not getting a direct answer. So, what is it? What's this greatest secret?"

"The greatest secret in the universe," Gideon slowly repeated, "is actually not a secret at all. It's something almost everyone knows instinctively, but most people never quite know it in their hearts. It's one thing to *know about* something and an entirely different matter to *know* that thing. The greatest secret is really the most open secret of all. It's written in almost all scriptures, but because humanity loves to complicate simple ideas, it has been overlooked time and time again. To tell the..."

"Oh come on, Gideon," I interrupted, "just spell it out."

"And that's another thing," he said in a most commanding tone, "patience is one of your areas that could use a little improvement, John. Learn to be patient and you'll hear the rhythm of the universe."

"I'm sorry. Please go on," I said in a guilt-ridden tone.

"Develop a close and personal relationship with God and everything else will fall into place. That's the greatest secret of the entire universe, of all time. Simple, isn't it? I told you it was such an open secret, so simple that most people won't believe it. Well, there you have it. And don't forget, this can only be done from within."

I looked at him scarcely believing what I had heard. *That* was the secret? After all this time waiting for Gideon to explain the greatest secret in the universe and have him tell me that all I had to do was to develop a close personal relationship with God was more than I could take. How absurd! I began laughing out loud and found that it was becoming more difficult to stop. Finally Marla's voice broke through my laughter. "What's so funny, John?" she asked, "I don't see anything funny about it at all."

Looking at her I saw there wasn't even a remote trace of amusement on her face. I composed myself while replying, "It's downright funny, Marla. To think that I believed anyone could know the greatest secret. How could I ever have believed such a thing? Well, you're both great. You certainly did put one over on me. I should have known there was no such thing."

Gideon and Marla looked at each other as if to say that this conversation was getting nowhere. I obviously didn't think they were serious. Yet, they had never given me false information before. They were always truthful, though there were times when they did not choose to explain everything. I was a bit more serious now. "Gideon," I said, "you *are* joking, aren't you?"

"No, I'm not joking," he said.

"So, this is the tremendous, big secret?" I mused.

"I imagine, John, that it would have had more of an awesome effect on you if ten thousand angels, complete with blaring trumpets, descended in a blinding, brilliant flash of light to present it to you. And better still, if these envoys disguised it in a thousand mysterious puzzles or enigmatic phrases, it would be easier for you to accept than the simple, honest way I presented it to you. To discover truth, most people want to believe that mysterious quests must be made through obscure mazes only to discover complex messages disguised in a multiplicity of meanings. They feel that they must search for hidden scriptures or lost tablets, magic crystals or the Ambrose Stone. Why is it, John, that people will believe the most absurd ideas when those ideas are made to seem complex beyond comprehension. Yet, they will ignore the most profound ideas presented with simplicity and clarity?" Gideon shook his head, as if puzzled.

"It must be, Gideon, that some things just seem too simple to be true. This secret you just told me seems like simplicity itself... too easy. It's as if, well, don't get me wrong, but it really seems as if anyone could do it... develop a close personal relationship with the Almighty—Ha! What's so special about that? Don't we all have that sort of relationship already? And look at how much good it's done for humanity."

"I suppose you believe that's God's fault?" Gideon asked. "Someone once said, 'God is simple. All else is complex.' Yes, of course, it's simplicity itself, but within its simplicity are powers too majestic and invincible to comprehend. Let me put it another way. When there's a relationship of absolute trust between you and your God, many things start to happen. For example, you'll find that your life seems to have more meaning, that you're much stronger and more peaceful than before and that you don't whine and complain as much as you used to. You'd be happier than you've ever been and other people would seek you out just to be in your company."

Sitting here on the porch with my two other-worldly friends reminded me of a similar visit long ago. "Haven't we discussed these things before?" I asked.

With a smile of forbearance, Marla said, "Many times, John, many times. Each time we discuss this idea you understand a bit more than the time before. Perhaps, this time you'll get the meaning of the whole concept. Enlightenment doesn't always come with a brilliant flash of lightning or the exploding rumble of thunder. It's more evolutionary than revolutionary. Sometimes it creeps up ever so slowly, ever so gently, takes you by the hand and says, 'Come with me, I'll show you wonders undreamed of and I'll give you peace and happiness unheard of.' Enlightenment says there are no beginnings, no endings only a state of being. Remember the birds and the books in your dream?"

"You mean when I was a little boy? The dream about the birds under the mango tree? You know about that, huh?" I waited for her answer, but Gideon replied instead.

"We know many things, John. Every beginning appears to lead to an ending, but then again, every so-called ending implies a new beginning. So, really there are no beginnings nor endings, just the ongoing process of life. We use beginnings and endings as markers and reference points and, as such, they may be of some small use. But the highway of life is endless and the journey is much more exciting when one really knows the secret—the simple secret of living life to its fullest. That was precisely what was written in the unfamiliar language in the book you found under the tree in your dream."

"What you're saying then is that life is a strange and beautiful process and that we really can enjoy this journey without much suffering, problems or hardship?"

"Absolutely. Yes," replied Gideon.

I continued, "I feel I've always known that and, yet, I couldn't believe it because my life has been far from simple and certainly not problem-free. This secret of life that you speak of, Gideon, I am familiar with it. But really, has it done me any good? Has my life been much better because I knew this secret? Furthermore, I believe lots of people know that secret and, yet, I don't think it's done them much good, either. So what's the use?"

"Being in possession of information is one thing. Doing something with that information is another matter altogether. You're right, John," continued Gideon, "absolutely right. Many know the secret. But few do anything with it. They prefer to sit back, to moan and whine about the injustices of life. They don't seem to have enough courage to take a chance on life, to do something with their lives. They'd rather be spectators than participants in the great game of life."

"And what's wrong with being spectators instead of participants, Gideon? Have you noticed, it's the players on the field who get awfully banged up and bloody?"

"There's nothing, absolutely nothing wrong, except the spectators don't get the same rewards as the participants. That's all. The funniest thing, though, is that we're all participants and spectators at the same time. It's just a variation on a point of view. Do something with the greatest secret in the universe and it will work for you. Stare at a monster long enough and you begin to become more like a monster. Associate and be close to God more often and you begin to become god-like. Being close to God has nothing to do with time and space. It has to do with awareness. You have to be constantly aware of this closeness and always feel the safety and security of being there."

"I know you don't mean that I'll have a problem-free existence," I said, "but it shouldn't always be so hard. Everyday isn't meant to be a struggle for survival, eking out a meager living just to barely exist in despair and sadness. Sometimes the road is so long and the way so dark... ."

Marla wouldn't let me finish. "We've heard that song many times before. Let's not go over it again, John. Of course, the road could be long and the way dark. But there are tools available to deal with long roads and dark ways. Keep moving on and the road becomes shorter. Stay in the light and the darkness disappears. How do you do that? A close, personal relationship with the Chief, the God of all creation. There is nothing extraordinary about all this. It's not that your problems will be less difficult. What will happen is that you'll become much stronger, much more capable of dealing with the difficulties of life. You'll live your life from a much higher point of view."

"Sure, John," said Gideon, "it's not always easy, but no one ever said this Earth journey was going to be easy. As they say, 'they never promised you a rose garden.' But then again, the way I figure it, if you want the roses, you've got to put up with the thorns. If you want the highs of living, you've got to deal with the lows of life. Yet, by keeping close to the Almighty, the highs can become higher and the lows aren't nearly as low as you once believed."

"You both have been very patient with me," I said. "You've shared many gems of wisdom over the years. Now you've told me the greatest secret in the universe and I'm very, very grateful. But I'm still a bit confused. I know that to live a life of joy, peace and fulfillment, one must develop a close, personal relationship with God. And I believe that this is true. But one thing you haven't told me. How does one develop this relationship? How do you get to the point where this relationship becomes a natural thing in your life? Where do you start and how do you continue?"

"Like everything else, there are some simple rules," Gideon replied. "Why don't we get a cup of that great coffee you usually make? Then we'll be able to go over how to develop some good habits—how to always be in the Presence of the Protector—how to always find safety, security and prosperity. Fair enough?"

"I can't argue with that, Gideon. It'll only take a few minutes to make the brew. Marla, would you like some fruit juice?"

"If you don't mind, I'll take coffee, John. There are times when I enjoy a steaming cup of the stuff. Do you need some help getting it together?"

"No thanks, I think I can handle it."

They remained seated while I went to the kitchen and put on the coffee. Now I'll find out all about the greatest secret in the universe. At last, I'll learn how to use it to full advantage to fill my life with more joy than drudgery, more contentment than anxiety, more love than fear.

Chapter Eighteen

In Trailing Clouds of Glory

"I see you remembered to plug in the coffeepot," Gideon quipped when I returned.

"What do you mean?" I asked.

"Well, not too long ago, a friend of yours was visiting and you offered to make him some coffee. You couldn't figure out why it was taking so long until finally your friend noticed that you had forgotten to plug in the coffeepot. Then there was the time when you forgot to fill the pot with water. Do you want me to continue?"

"No," I laughed. "I guess I'm like the absent-minded professor. Those were just minor over-sights. In the big picture, they're lost in the fabric. Let's get on with more meaningful things—like how does one get closer to God?"

"Marla," Gideon winked at her, "I've never seen him so anxious to learn. Have you?"

"I can feel his enthusiasm, Gideon," she answered. "I think, if he pays attention, what he learns here today might stay with him for the rest of his life. But let's not keep him waiting."

And thus I was granted a legacy of wisdom that was to serve me well ever after. "In the first place," Gideon stated, "God is not a person, a place, a time or a thing to be found. God is everywhere, everywhen and everything. God is the Presence that pervades every part of the universe from the largest star down to the tiniest atom. When you become aware, looking for God is like a fish searching for water. You'll know that you don't ever have to search because you've always been surrounded by God's Presence."

"I remember, years ago, hearing something like that from God Himself or Herself. It must have been another one of those dreams that seemed so real."

"That wasn't a dream, John. God spoke directly to you and explained some of these things. You probably have just forgotten."

"God spoke to me? I'd never forget if God spoke to me."

Somehow, Gideon's patience and understanding reminded me of my dad. "God speaks to everyone, John, but not all hear Him. And those who do hear are likely to forget because they rationalize and analyze too much. Most of them don't think they're worthy of God speaking directly to them. That guilt or self-worth thing again, you see. What with all those preachers spewing fire and brimstone from their pulpits, one can well imagine how difficult it is to hear the still, small voice of God.

"God loves us because it's God's nature to love. God doesn't only love us, God *is* love. He wants us to be aware of this love and to know that we could never be separated from His Presence.

There was a moment of silence, then Gideon continued. "Practice the Presence of God and you'll feel His Spirit, strength and love within you. It doesn't matter what religion you follow. You don't even have to be a member of any special group to do this. Anyone can do it. You don't have to believe it to do it, either. If you practice often enough, it'll become a part of you. You'll start believing it to be true and after believing, you'll start knowing it to be true."

Gideon jumped in again. "We've now given you all the tools you need, John. Our work with you is almost over."

"What?" I objected, "you're acting as if I won't be seeing you again. Is that what you mean?" I felt sadness enfolding me as I considered the possibility of not seeing my two friends again.

"Certainly not, John. No such luck. Now you'll see us whenever you want to see us," said Marla. "Just hold us strongly in your thoughts and, in a short while, we'll bump into each other."

"Never forget," said Gideon, "that the magic is not only in you, but all around you. This Universe is a magical Universe and was designed for our enjoyment and growth. *You change your world by changing the way you look at it. It's all a matter of perception and attitudes.* We'll meet whenever you want to and chat about things that are important to you. Call on either or both of us and we'll be there. From now on, so long as you always remember that the Presence is with you, your life will flow in trailing clouds of glory from God Who is your home."

"How about some more coffee?" I offered. I was so overwhelmed, it was all I could think of saying at the moment.

"No, thank you," said Gideon.

"Not for me, either," replied Marla.

Suddenly it had become extremely still around us. Not even a whisper in the wind could be heard.

Without warning, the detonating sound of thunder exploded. Instinctively I blinked and in that split-second I found myself alone, holding my half-empty cup of coffee. Gideon and Marla had vanished. I rose from my seat and walked into the kitchen. There, in the sink, I found their coffee cups. Somewhat awe-struck, I stood staring at nothing in particular. "In trailing clouds of glory. . . ." The words echoed through the hallways and ricocheted off the walls of my mind as I went about preparing - dinner.

Now, dear reader, as you and I arrive at this point, perhaps, it's a good time to consider, without a doubt, that each of us has been led here to reflect on this simple truth — ***Although our beginnings may end and our endings begin again, throughout all eternity we will be "journeying" in the everlasting Fields of Forever.***

~~ A Note from the Author~~

If you have enjoyed *Journey in the Fields of Forever*, you may want to read *The Power Pause—3 Minutes, 3-Steps to Real Success and Personal Happiness*.

The *Power Pause* is written in story form and contains, in simple language, all that I've learned from Gideon and Marla in my travels through this dimension. It teaches you how, in only three minutes and using three steps, you can dramatically change your life from existing to living. To find out more about the *Power Pause*, go to http://www.powerpause.com

Journey in the Fields of Forever is the third in the series of adventures with Gideon and Marla. If you have not yet read the first in the series, *When You Can Walk on Water, Take the Boat*, youll find it on amazon.com

The second book in the series is called, *Morning Has Been All Night Coming*. This, too is at the amazon.com online bookstore

Thank you for joining me in these glorious adventures. Perhaps we shall meet again in future books. May your life be filled with all good things.

Much love and many blessings.

-- John Harricharan

Made in the USA
San Bernardino,
CA

58886068R00129